How to
Complete
a
Nightmare

How to Complete a Nightmare

*Responding Creatively to
Disturbing Dreams*

LEN WORLEY, Ph.D.

How to Complete a Nightmare:
Responding Creatively to Disturbing Dreams
Published by EVOLUTIONARY DREAMING
Austin, Texas, U.S.A.

Cover image adapted from Illustration 222099135 © Halina Yermakova | Dreamstime.com

Book Design by Michelle M. White

Library of Congress Control Number: 2021923018

WORLEY, LEN, Author
HOW TO COMPLETE A NIGHTMARE
LEN WORLEY, Ph.D.

ISBN: 979-8-9852910-0-1

BODY, MIND & SPIRIT / Dreams
SELF-HELP / Post-Traumatic Stress Disorder (PTSD)
PSYCHOLOGY / Movements / Jungian

QUANTITY PURCHASES:
Schools, companies, professional groups, clubs, and other organizations may qualify for special terms when ordering quantities of this title.
For information, email evolutionarydreaming@gmail.com.

This book is printed in
The United States of America.

This book is dedicated to:

Evelyn, my mother,
whose disturbing dreams,
suffered with great sincerity,
initiated my search.

And to Jasmine,
who taught me like no other
that nightmares,
when faced and understood,
can make us strong.

Above all, we must realize that active imagination is hard
work . . . We undertake it in order to open negotiations
with everything that is unknown in our psyche. Whether
we know it or not, our whole peace of mind depends
on these negotiations; otherwise, we are forever a house
divided against itself, distressed without knowing why,
and very insecure because something unknown in us
is constantly opposing us.

It is therefore of the utmost importance to feel friendly
to the idea that there is a great deal of a personal nature,
and still more of an impersonal one, that we do not know
and which continues to exert a compelling effect upon us.
Once we realize...that this is a fact which we cannot alter,
there is really no reason not to feel friendly towards it.
If fate obliges us to live with a companion or companions
whom we would not have chosen for ourselves, it is
obvious that life will go much more smoothly if we
turn a friendly, rather than hostile, face towards them.

BARBARA HANNAH (1981), ENCOUNTERS WITH THE SOUL

La Sabiduría Consuela al Soñador
(Wisdom Consoles the Dreamer)
by Tenaz (Ecuador)

Contents

The
Problem of
Nightmares

I am intimately acquainted with disturbing dreams. As far back as I remember and throughout my childhood, they awakened me in the middle of the night. But they were not my own. Jarred out of sleep by screams from another room, I would panic, certain an intruder had entered our home. But after a moment of collecting myself, I would realize, "Oh, she's having another nightmare."

Being the concerned boy that I was and wanting relief from the chilling high-pitched voice that pierced the night's sanctity ("Help! Help! Please help me!"), I would find my way through our darkened house and stand at the door of my parents' bedroom. Inside, my mother was anguishing, desperate for relief as she attempted to escape something or someone who pursued her. My father had profound hearing loss and would have taken his hearing aids out before bed, so he slept quietly beside my mother, undisturbed.

At first, I would gently knock on the bedroom door while softly calling out to my mother. I did not want to add to her panic by breaking into her sleep abruptly. I gradually increased my volume: "mom. Mom, MOM!" until she found her way back to safety. I would then explain as comfortingly as a boy could, "You were dreaming."

Confounded by these disturbing events, which happened more times than I can recall, I would sometimes linger, perplexed by the horrific experience my mother had just suffered, and I would ask, "What were you dreaming?"

Two themes dominated her nightmares. "A man was after me," she would explain, and though I was too young to understand the implications in my early years, I came to realize that my mother feared that she was about to be raped. The second theme of my mother's dreams was even more upsetting: "The snake, Len," she would grimly say. "It's that snake again."

I grew up in a fundamentalist Christian family and was taught at home and church that Adam and Eve were our first parents and were deceived by an evil serpent, causing the downfall of the human race. Standing there at my parents' bedroom door, I was baffled and disquieted. As a child in this religious environment, there was something foreboding about the serpent being in our house.

I do not recall exactly when the words formed in me, but a question lingered with me for many years: "Why was a dangerous stranger chasing my mother, and what did that terrible serpent want?"

I am not sure if my mother ever even asked this question, but I do know that she continued to suffer these nightly outcries into her mid-eighties, even weeks before she died. As you will read, these early dreams of my mother had a profound impact on me, motivating me to finally come to terms with them in the last chapter of this book: Why Did the Serpent Chase My Mother?

I did not realize how pivotal these childhood experiences were for me for many years. It was only after I had been trained as a psychologist that I came upon a passage from the Swiss psychiatrist Carl Jung that caused me to realize that fate had posed a question to me in my early life.

> . . . I became aware of the fateful links between me and my ancestors. I feel very strongly that I am under the influence of things or questions which were left incomplete by my parents and grandparents and more distant ancestors. It often seems as if there was an impersonal karma within a family that is passed on from parents to children. It has always seemed to me that I had to answer questions which fate had posed to my forefathers, and which had not yet been answered, or as if I had to complete, and perhaps continue, things which previous generations had left unfinished (Jung, 1989, p. 233).

I discovered this passage in my early forties, about ten years after becoming a psychologist and just a couple of years after having had the great fortune of meeting the woman who became my therapist, Sukie Colegrave, who skillfully helped me work with hundreds of my own dreams, many of which were nightmarish. I was astounded at the wisdom available in my dreams once I found someone who could help me discern their meaning. Up until then, I had always been curious about dreams, but I had remained as confused and bewildered about them as I was when I stood at my parents' bedroom door.

Finally able to discern the intention of my dreams with the help of my therapist, I started recalling my dreams with much greater frequency. To my chagrin and surprise, I discovered that many of them were disturbing. Yes, there were a great many alluring, erotic, and enchanting dreams that I hated to see end, but just as often, I had frightening dreams. As I began to listen to the dreams of my clients and close friends, I found that many of their dreams were also unsettling. As I would learn, disturbing dreams increase in frequency when someone is experiencing stressful life events, but even without undue stress, most people have threatening elements in their dreams well over half the time (Revonsuo, 2000). Given that we adults, on average, dream two hours each night, that's a lot of disturbance to be lived through in a lifetime! And the situation is much worse for someone who has been traumatized.

Trauma and Nightmares

It is common for someone with post-traumatic stress disorder (PTSD) to have disruptive dreams. As most trauma sufferers know, as well as those who sleep beside them, nightmares are one of the most hellish aspects of traumatic experience, often resulting in chronic sleep deprivation and an unnerving, unrelenting re-experiencing of the original trauma. For this reason, those with PTSD understandably just want their nightmares to stop. But here is the dilemma. It is difficult to stop dreaming.

It takes a lot of alcohol, cannabis, or a strong pharmaceutical to disrupt a process that Nature has invested a great amount of effort in us having (again, two hours of dreaming each night). Furthermore, sleep and dream research (Walker, 2017) tell us that the stage of sleep when most dreaming occurs, rapid eye movement (REM), is a highly beneficial, intelligent, restorative process. So much good comes from it: memory consolidation (similar to moving data from temporary storage to a more permanent file), emotional regulation (lessening anxiety and depression), and enhanced creativity in problem-solving, to name just a few of the documented benefits of REM and dreaming.

But if you have PTSD and chronically suffer nightmares, as a great percentage of traumatized people do, it is difficult to imagine any good coming from dreaming. Desperate to find relief, you would understandably do almost anything to have a good night's sleep and be relieved of the constant reminder of past trauma. The problem is that dreaming is deeply encoded in human experience, and not only in us. Practically all mammals dream. It is virtually impossible to extinguish dreaming. "But why," I have asked myself, "must dreams be so disturbing?"

Despite having been exposed to my mother's nightmares early on and having worked with a few thousand dreams as a psychologist, my own and those of others, I must say that I am surprised I never confronted this issue: Why do we have nightmares? Given that they are so unnerving, and for people with PTSD so disruptive, what is the purpose of these terrifying events? Or is there a purpose? Perhaps like many medical professionals and laypeople suppose, nightmares result from a disordered or faulty mechanism in the brain or personality, like corrupted software. Or, in the case of PTSD, perhaps nightmares are simply the result of damage done by trauma, and they must simply be endured.

The question of WHY we have nightmares didn't concern me for many years. I was curious about them, probably more than most, given my early experience with them as a child, but I had never taken them on as my issue or my question to resolve. This changed when I fell in love with someone who suffered from PTSD.

It has always been moving for me to hear a client tell me a disturbing dream that happened a few nights or weeks ago, but my empathy for nightmare sufferers was increased a hundredfold as the result of being awakened by someone I love who was lying beside me filled with anguish from a disturbing dream that had catapulted her back into reliving past trauma. Few things have been more riveting for me than holding my beloved's trembling body in the middle of the night when I attempted to console her as she emerged from yet another dream that brought to mind the past horror she had endured.

Seeing up close and firsthand how terrible the anguish is that is stirred through trauma dreams, a commitment finally arose from the depths of me one night. "No more!" I declared. "No more will I passively witness the suffering that ensues when someone is caught in a nightmare!" I resolutely decided to find a solution, undoubtedly building on my early childhood experiences with my mother. "What can be done?" I demanded! "Must someone resign themselves to enduring nightmares nightmares for the rest of their life or at least until the underlying trauma is resolved, which at best may take years to resolve?" Love compelled me to say, "No! This cannot be." Thus began my search in earnest to understand disturbing dreams in a way that relief could be found.

Unexpected Solutions

What I discovered surprised me, both in its simplicity and brevity. Nightmares, whether associated with trauma or not, can be stopped or at least altered in such a way that they lose their disturbing impact. Not only that, this can happen in much less time than most would ever expect. You will read about this in the chapter: *The Crucial Step.* In short, a method called Image Rehearsal Therapy (Krakow & Zadra, 2010) combines simple breath and relaxation training with directions to write an alternative narrative that is less frightening. Crucial to the success of this straightforward approach is that the dreamer must then rehearse the new dream scenario (while awake) numerous times over the following days. Surprisingly, most people, the great majority in fact, who complete this brief process have dramatically fewer and less severe nightmares, if they reoccur at all.

Once I learned of Image Rehearsal Therapy, I thought my search was over—what a relief. Yet, as I reviewed many of my nightmares and the wisdom that ensued from having investigated them—not having attempted to simply make them stop—I realized that I would have suffered a significant loss had I not learned the valuable lessons they brought. Many people feel this way about their dreams. Even though discomforting, if not outright frightening, many intuit that there is a purpose to their dreams, especially if they are riveting, and they thus feel compelled to understand the reasons for their nightmares, not just stop them from reoccurring. In truth, the meanings I have found in my dreams have been life-changing.

I began to wonder: Might Nature have something in mind when it orchestrates these difficult experiences for us? Are they as haphazard as many people believe? In other words, is there something intentional about a nightmare? Even if it is difficult to experience, might it come to help us? If this is the case, how do we go about discerning a nightmare's purpose and cooperating with it to thus benefit from what Nature intended?

Such ideas have profound implications, especially when considering dreams related to trauma. For example, if nightmares not only occur because of trauma but also to help us heal trauma, then we must do a roundabout turn and approach nightmares quite differently.

For starters, we must show them respect. And from there, we must approach them with greater curiosity, not idle, intellectual speculation. Most of all, if indeed nightmares are created by Nature to help us, perhaps we can learn to trust them, and thus look for the good in them, even when we are unnerved by them, considering that perhaps an intelligent, purposeful process is at work, one that might even be working on our behalf. These are radical ideas, I know, but what if there is actually a benevolent process at work in our dreaming? If this is the case, we could form a different relationship with our dreams. Rather than avoid or rationalize them away ("It was only a dream."), we could turn towards them, even when we have initially felt disgust, and study them to see if indeed they intend to help us.

Chased by the Very Thing I Needed

To illustrate how nightmares may be attempting to help us, I will share a decisive dream I had in my late thirties. It remains one of my most important dreams, not only because of how frightening it was—I feared I was about to be killed—but also because the dream taught me valuable lessons about myself and the evolutionary function of dreaming.

At the time of the dream, I had been working as a psychologist for several years, and I must admit that while I thought I was mature and developed in my personality, I now see that I had deficits in my capacity to be authentic and close with friends and a romantic partner. However, I knew nothing of this until a dream brought this humbling realization to my awareness.

The dream started with me dreaming that I was in bed asleep. I am awakened by the sound of the window to my bedroom being abruptly opened.

Startled, I look to my right and see an African bushman, clothed only in a loincloth and holding a spear in his right hand, climbing through the raised window. Alarmed, I reach for a shotgun that had been given to me when I was a teenager, which I just happened to have in bed with me (yes, dreams are seemingly weird and nonsensical at first). I aim and shoot the intruder who falls to the floor, but as soon as he collapses, another robust masculine warrior climbs in. Again, I kill the second man, but to my dismay, a third bushman crawls through my window. Upon shooting him, a fourth man enters, dressed like the others and with the same pointed spear. I then despair, knowing that there will be no end to the stream of these fierce men finding their way into my house.

I told my dream to my therapist, who was well-versed in the psychology of Carl Jung. She considered that dream figures may be symbolic of hidden potentials of the personality that are ready to be actualized. However, she reminded me that if we were not allowed to develop certain strengths earlier in life, their appearance in dreams (in symbolic form) might indeed be intimidating.

In my case, I had never developed a robust masculine capacity to set boundaries and defend myself in the way that my invading warriors could. My early life was oriented to pleasing, accommodating, and being a dutiful, obedient child due to being raised in a strict, fundamentalist, authoritarian church and home. Essentially, I had never learned to speak up for myself, even though I was an educated man. Of course, I had opinions about life and could advise others in my psychology practice, but when it came to expressing disagreements in friendships and negotiating differences, especially with a romantic partner, I feared conflict. When bothered, I withdrew and became emotionally distant rather than expressing myself. As you might imagine, this strategy of avoiding conflict prevented deep friendships from forming and dampened emotional intimacy.

The warriors epitomized a quality I desperately needed, but until the dream, I had no awareness of this. These men were unafraid and carried spears that enabled them to stand their ground, defend themselves, and thus maintain their safety and integrity. Having an encounter with them had a profound effect on me once I understood the intention of their appearance. No amount of advice from friends or professionals telling me that I needed to speak up for myself would have been as compelling or riveting as these primal warriors breaking into my bedroom.

You will read more about this dream in later chapters and see the methods of dream investigation I used that helped me find life-changing insights for myself. But for now, I wish to convey how some dream figures that at first appear harmful to us may actually symbolize the very qualities that are missing and needed for us to be more fully functioning human beings.

I must also add here that not all threatening dream figures represent qualities that could be useful for us. Some may be reflections of internalized attitudes of self-hate, self-indulgence, or self-inflation (being "too full of ourselves") that are unknowingly undermining us. In these cases, dreams serve the function much like an x-ray, revealing underlying conditions that compromise our health and vitality. Such dreams are humbling encounters with the unknown (but influential) life-limiting parts of ourselves.

As you will read, there are enormous benefits in being able to discern when a frightening dream figure is revealing negative aspects of yourself, or instead is providing a picture of undeveloped qualities (like my warriors) which are essential to evolving you into a more robust version of what you could be.

The Evolutionary Function of Dreaming

There is a central theme repeated throughout the various stories you will find in this book. I have come to believe that dreams, and nightmares, in particular, are attempts by Nature to evolve us into becoming wiser, more skillful, and better prepared for the ongoing challenges we face during life on earth. My dream of robust bushmen illustrates this evolutionary function. Nature pushes us through the dreaming process to grow into what we have never been, someone more capable of meeting the demands of life. However, if we do not understand this intense and challenging process, we will overlook and misinterpret difficult dreams and thus delay our development.

What I have just asserted in the above paragraph is by no means commonly accepted. In fact, in Lena Sayed's (2011) scholarly review of the current theories on dreaming, she makes clear how divided the scientific field is about the purpose of dreaming. Some theorists propose that we dream to consolidate memories, to retain what we have learned the previous day. Others argue that dreaming regulates emotions, lessening the extremes of anxiety and depression. Some theorists propose that dreaming enables us to be more creative in solving the problems of waking life, while others maintain that dreaming serves a therapeutic purpose, providing psychological wisdom. At the same time, there are those who believe that dreams are not inherently meaningful at all but rather are stories created by the waking mind to make sense of chaotic images formed by what are only random firings of the brain during sleep.

Drawing on dream researcher Rosalind Cartwright (2000), Sayed (2011) likens the conflicting ideas about the function of dreams to the story of the blind men who described what an elephant is like based on each one's perception of only one part of the large animal. I agree. It seems that dreaming is like a stage where various activities can occur. Theatrical events as diverse as comedy or tragedy can be performed, graduation ceremonies conducted, symphonies played, and political speeches given. The janitor may enter late at night and clean this same stage of debris. Likewise, many functions can be performed in dreaming, and as of yet, there is no agreement about any single theory that unites them all. Perhaps it is even too much to expect that a unifying theory could be found.

In my mind, one theory comes close to providing an overarching explanation of the function of dreaming, at least the threatening aspect of disturbing dreams, and we likely share this same function with dogs, cats, and many other animals. The Threat Simulation Theory by Finnish neuroscientist Antti Revonsuo (2000) proposes that we have evolved the capacity to simulate adverse scenarios during sleep to give us practice at recognizing and avoiding threats in waking life. We dream of distressing events to sharpen our ability to protect ourselves. I remember having an idea similar to this long before I learned of Revonsuo's work when I looked inside the cockpit of a flight simulator at Kennedy Space Center in Florida. I was struck by its similarity with dreaming.

During flight simulations, would-be astronauts and pilots are exposed to various challenging situations they are likely to face in real-time flight. A primary purpose of these simulations is to make participants aware of their weak spots and then challenge them repeatedly until they develop mastery of potentially life-threatening situations.

Revonsuo (2000), the leading theorist on dreams as a simulation experience, proposes that our dreams contain threatening events because we retain an ancient mechanism that enables us to rehearse the detection and avoidance of dangerous events. In his view, it is enough to fight or flee a threatening situation in a dream because this helps maintain the integrity of the survival system. I like Revonsuo's theory because it suggests how dreaming may have first evolved. However, it seems to me that many other functions of dreaming have developed as the human brain has changed. I have encountered many dreams that appear to be asking more of the dreamer than simply fighting, fleeing, or freezing to avoid harm. In fact, it seems to me that habitually resorting to such emergency strategies in our dreams may be what causes nightmares to continue, especially for someone with PTSD. I will say more about this in the chapter *The Crucial Step*.

I think much more is at play for us humans in dreaming than merely maintaining our protective instincts. My dream of the primal warriors, along with countless other threatening dreams I have investigated, tells me that Nature attempts to help us become more nuanced and skillful in how we respond to threat, not just highly reactive like I was when I shot the men invading my bedroom. As you will read, I believe that Nature pushes us through dreaming to become masterful in dealing with the challenges of waking life. Dreaming may bring us face to face with disavowed potentials (like my warriors) that are ready to be actualized, and it sometimes brings us to humbling awareness of forces in our personalities that undermine us and make us weak, all for the purpose of making us strong.

It appears that Nature places a high value on us responding accurately to the demands of the present moment without being caught in overreactive strategies like fight, flight, or freeze that may have been useful in an emergency but no longer serve us once the threatening situation is over. Being overly aggressive, avoidant, or freezing in the presence of something threatening, may actually endanger us in waking life.

Therefore, I believe that one of the primary functions of dreams, especially after a traumatizing event, is to provide rehearsal time so that we can develop more creative and masterful responses to threatening scenarios and thus not be stuck in highly reactive behaviors. But to accomplish this, we must do more than endure dreadful dreams. We must become proactive in how we deal with threats. As you will see, making a creative response to difficult dreams is at the heart of the nightmare completion process.

What is Nightmare Completion?

As suggested in the title Nightmare **Completion**, I believe there is something incomplete, unfinished about a distressing dream. It is as if a dramatic story has prematurely ended. A dream may leave us in a defeated position, having succumbed to an overwhelming force, or it may leave us uncertain if we have outrun the villain from which we have tried to escape. Nightmares characteristically end in tragedy.

From an evolutionary perspective, I believe that these difficult encounters serve a purpose: to elicit a creative response from us. For this reason, we should not ignore a difficult dream. Upon waking, we can study our actions to see how we did not act with wisdom and courage. From here, we can thus re-imagine an ending to the drama whereby we are skillful rather than highly reactive or victimized. A creative response may also entail discerning the nature of threatening dream figures: do they symbolize qualities that can help us (like my skillful warriors), or do they represent attitudes or behaviors that undermine our success in the world?

Here is the good news. As you will read in the stories of many dreamers throughout this book, when we find a creative response to recurrent nightmares that is unique and authentic for our particular personality, they cease, or at least lose their disturbing intensity, since their intended purpose is satisfied. This is what it means to complete a nightmare.

Here are the essential components of this process, which I will explain in detail in subsequent chapters:

Step 1 – Establish a feeling of safety within yourself. It is important to learn to relax enough to study a difficult dream. Otherwise, your defenses will be so high that you will not be able to find a creative response to your disturbing dreams. It is not necessary to do away with anxiety. You only need to feel safe enough to remain steady and courageous to face what is difficult. The nightmare completion process utilizes simple but potent practices to induce a feeling of safety.

Step 2 – Take the Crucial Step. Stopping, facing, and writing a nightmare in detail is undoubtedly the single most important intervention you can make to change frightening dreams. For this reason, this one simple act is called The Crucial Step. Though taking this step is usually the most difficult, it is also potentially the most rewarding because it satisfies one of the fundamental intentions of disturbing dreams: moving beyond the highly reactive strategies of fight, flight, or freeze.

Step 3 – Make a Creative Response. If you study your behavior in a nightmare, you will often see that you are over or under-reactive. You may become intimidated and run away, or conversely, become highly aggressive, attempting to kill off what is threatening to you. Sometimes you may freeze. It is possible to go back into your dream, once awake, and re-write the dream by adding scenes, creating conversations with dream figures to discover why they acted as they did, and, in general, re-script your dream so that you are acting in the dream more masterfully. There is no limit to the kinds of creative responses you can make; however, they typically include one of the following:

- Moving from Actor to Director. This involves crafting a revised version of a disturbing dream that shows you responding to threats with mastery, resulting in you feeling empowered rather than victimized.

- Absorbing Difficult Truths. Dreams may sober us with realizations of how we have been hurt or have harmed others. We benefit when honestly facing reality, especially when we do so with humility and compassion.

- Knowing Your Adversary. Not all dream figures that frighten us intend to do us harm. This is probably THE most misunderstood dynamic of dreaming. Threatening dream figures often represent hidden potentials and personality strengths that were not allowed earlier in life but are now ready to be actualized.

- Realizing Undermining Influences. As medical imagining can reveal disease processes within the body, dreams may show psychological forces in the personality that are harmful and undermining us. These may appear as abusive dream figures, representing internalized attitudes of self-hate, or we may encounter self-indulgent characters who lack moral constraint. Such off-putting dreams can safeguard us by alerting us to underlying tendencies within us that can potentially be harmful to ourselves or others.

• Advocating for the Helpless. We can go back into a dream (once awake, when re-writing the narrative) and intervene on behalf of someone vulnerable. We can step in front of an abuser and stop exploitation. We can speak up on behalf of a person in a weak position (including ourselves). We can confront someone who is being aggressive and investigate why they are hostile towards us.

Step 4 – Rehearse the creative response. Reliving your creative response to a nightmare is essential in nightmare completion. Studies show that rehearsing your newfound response sets in motion healing forces within the personality (Krakow & Zadra, 2006/2010). This may involve simply reading the new version of your dream several times a day and thus experiencing yourself in a non-victimized, empowered role. Or it may involve changing attitudes and behaviors in waking life as a result of insights found in your dream. Remembering a dream in this way enables new parts of the self to take root and grow.

By summarizing the Nightmare Completion process into the above four steps, I am not suggesting it is easy. On the contrary, completing a nightmare can be emotionally challenging, for it often involves turning and facing difficult emotions which have been avoided for a long while. Throughout this book, the stories of real dreamers will give examples of how others have faced what is difficult and crafted creative responses to their troubling dreams.[1] Hopefully, this will serve as inspiration to you to do the same.

---

1. The dreams I have quoted throughout this book remain as they were told to me. However, I have changed the biographical details of all dreamers to protect their privacy, with the exception of my mother and myself.

The
Nightmare
Completion
Process

1

Establishing Safety
Within Yourself

I t is no small thing to face and study a nightmare because, in truth, disturbing dreams are connected to our most vulnerable feelings, and they are intimately tied to the core concerns of our lives. For this reason, dreams can be intimidating, causing many people to turn away, ignore, and attempt to forget them as soon as possible.

Investigating a nightmare requires courage. But not only that. We must feel safe enough to remain steady in the presence of what is difficult. For this reason, the first step in working with a nightmare is to establish a feeling of safety within yourself, but this by no means should imply that you wait until you lose all fear. All that is required is that you feel safe enough not to panic and run away in the presence of something that is intimidating. This, of course, is more easily said than done, and I assure you that there have been times that I have wanted to have nothing to do with a disturbing dream because the feelings of fear, shame, or regret have been so strong.

The ideas and practices that I share below have steadied me in the face of disturbing dreams, helping me overcome my inclination to turn away from difficult feelings. As a result of steading myself, I have been richly rewarded by discovering jewels of wisdom in what was initially simply a dream I wanted to forget.

Standing Your Ground

This first step of the nightmare completion process, *Establishing Safety*, could have just as easily been named *Standing Your Ground*, for indeed a certain gumption is required to investigate disturbing dreams. In one sense, you have to be willing to *take on* a dream, and *wrestle* with it, along with all the associated feelings, until a satisfying resolution can be found.

The idea of summoning your strength to face a dream came to me from psychiatrist Carl Jung. Serving as an inspiration to me, he used a word in the title of one chapter of his memoir that for years struck me as strange. He wrote of his experience with his own dreams as a **Confrontation** with the Unconscious. The German word translated as *confrontation*, *auseinandersetzung*, might also be rendered as "having it out with" or "coming to terms with," suggesting that we must struggle with a dream until it yields a valuable truth (Hannah, 1981).

The idea of *taking on a dream* will strike many as odd, as it did me initially. Before learning investigative methods of dreamwork, which I have described for you in this book, I approached dreams in an intellectually speculative way, only concerned with finding an explanation of why I had dreamed something. Little did I know that I had to work for valuable insights, and this often required that I turn and face difficult feelings.

A quote from Jung's memoir, *Memories, Dreams, Reflections* (1989), will illustrate how we must muscle up and tolerate disturbing feelings when facing unconscious forces inside ourselves. Here he describes how difficult it was for him at first to face feelings he had previously avoided.

> I was living in a constant state of tension; often, I felt as if gigantic blocks of stone were tumbling down upon me. One thunderstorm followed another. My enduring these storms was a question of brute strength. Others have been shattered by them... But there was a demonic strength in me, and from the beginning, there was no doubt in my mind that I must find the meaning of what I was experiencing in these fantasies. When I endured these assaults of the unconscious, I had an unswerving conviction that I was obeying a higher will, and that feeling continued to uphold me until I had mastered the task. (177)

Jung goes on to say that he would become so "wrought up" when he first started exploring his dreams that he had to do yoga exercises not to be overwhelmed.

> But since it was my purpose to know what was going on within myself, I would do these exercises only until I had calmed myself enough to resume my work with the unconscious. (177)

Here I believe Jung is referring to the practice of establishing safety within himself, and he did this not to banish difficult feelings but rather to calm himself enough to face and understand them.

If you already know how to calm yourself enough to study a difficult dream, you may wish to skip the remaining content in this chapter. However, if you are prone to ignore and dismiss difficult dreams, I suggest that you use one of the several practices I describe below to steady you enough to take on a nightmare, which is to stand your ground and investigate it so that it gives you valuable insights.

The Practice of Dual Awareness

In Nightmare Completion, we aim for dual awareness: to be calm and steady while also feeling anxious. You don't have to do away with the natural apprehension that arises when facing something difficult. The important thing is to remain calm enough so that you can tolerate challenging emotions. Doing so enables your innate creativity to find solutions and insights that can turn a nightmare into a source of wisdom. A personal example will help.

I sometimes imagine being on the back of a robust and healthy horse when I get afraid. My body, like the horse, is keyed up and ready to spring into action. If I am faced with an intensely intimidating situation, I can feel my urge to panic and run. Yet, another part of me knows that I must stay steady and face that which is challenging if I am to solve a problem. In such circumstances, I use the various practices I discuss below for calming myself so that my horse, my animal instinct, does not get spooked and run away. During such moments, I sometimes imagine offering words of reassurance to the horse under me, rubbing its neck and mane and consoling it with the soft tone of my voice so that it remains under my control, not panicked, and thus available to take me where and when I will need to go.

I have noticed that some people are astonished (and relieved) to discover that they can create a feeling of safety inside themselves. Before learning to do this, they may have lived their entire lives with an underlying restlessness, an apprehension that something bad will happen if they stop and relax. Indeed, the anticipation that something onerous will occur if you relax your guard is likely based on an accurate perception of the real dangers experienced earlier in life when the environment and the people in it were not safe. Such are the conditions of an abusive or neglectful home, school, and community. For this reason, anxiety is viewed respectfully in Nightmare Completion and not seen fundamentally as a disorder but rather an elegant signaling system that alerts us to danger. However, to benefit from this intelligent guidance, we must work with it rather than suppress and avoid it. We must steady ourselves enough so that we can listen to and study anxiety in order to perceive what the danger is and thus solve the problem that can potentially harm us.

Below I have listed some of the most reliable ways I have discovered for inducing a feeling of safety.

Purposeful Breathing

The breath is the most immediate way to change your nervous system from a hyper-aroused, anxious state to a calm one. When you breathe slightly slower and fuller than usual, you send a signal to your body's protective instincts that you are safe—we take rapid and shallow breaths when in a state of emergency. As a result, hormones and other chemical messengers are released, which bring you into calm and confidence. Breathing in an intentional way to evoke calm is one of the most tangible ways to affect body systems that generally are outside of conscious control: blood pressure, heartbeat, stress hormones.

However, it is not simply breathing more fully that matters. Breathing slightly slower than usual is the key, and especially if you breathe in such a way that you feel satisfied. It is the *satisfying feeling* of a *pleasurable* breath that helps the body switch out of a fight or flight response towards calm. Pleasure is the antidote to stress.

Yoga has evolved some potent ways of using the breath to calm the mind. *Alternate nostril breathing* can quickly induce relaxation (and give you a sense of control when anxious). Instructions for this can be easily found on a Google search. Also, you can extend the length of your in-breath and out-breath through counting. Additionally, breathing through the nose, at least during the in-breath, apparently has stronger neurological results than breathing in through the mouth. The so-called "ocean breath" (Ujjayi), used in some yoga practices, is a long, slow breath done by gently constricting the throat, causing a subtle ocean sound like you hear when you hold a seashell up to your ear. Ujjayi means "victorious" or "to conquer" and is an example of how breath can be used to both relax and build confidence at the same time.

I sometimes take a long, slow breath in and then purse my lips the way I would if I were directing my breath to "push" a candle flame away from me without blowing it out. The concentration required to bend the flame with such precision grows a feeling of mastery within, a sure antidote to feeling overwhelmed and out of control.

The bottom line on utilizing the breath is to bring awareness to it, watch it, then make it slightly fuller and slower than usual, and most of all, enjoy it so that you get out of your head and come into the pleasure of the animal body.

Staying Aware of the Body

Aside from using your breath to establish a feeling of safety, it is also helpful to become aware of sensations in your body. Where do you feel tension? You can breathe into that part of your body to signal the tissue to relax. Perhaps it will help to gently place your hand on tensed muscles as a gesture of consoling kindness, as if comforting yourself the way a kind mother comforts her child. (In fact, bearing the imagery of a consoling mother or friend in mind can also induce the relaxation response.) Being aware of how you are feeling in your body enables the mind to be more fully engaged in the present moment. Staying aware of how you are feeling in the body is particularly helpful if you have been traumatized and are remembering past hurts. Noticing and describing sensations in the body helps counter one of the primal emergency strategies we use when highly distressed: dissociation (leaving one's body).

Orienting to Where You Are

Another way to invoke safety is to orient yourself to your surroundings. Ask, "Am I safe here now?" Look around and be aware of where you are in the here and now, the room you are in, your house or building. Often we lose this primary orientation when we are caught up in a stress response, concentrating instead on the discomfort itself or preoccupying over past hurt or future danger. Reminding yourself that you are now safe and looking around to be sure this is so, as simple as this sounds, can establish a feeling of safety.

Intentional Movement

For some, relaxation practices, as mentioned above, may not be sufficient to make them feel safe. In fact, sitting still may at first engender more anxiety. Slow movement exercises may help instead, especially those that require the disciplined engagement of the body and breath. Yoga, Tai Chi, and Chi Kung necessitate being both relaxed and in control (but not over-controlling) at the same time, helping to strike a balance between the sympathetic (arousal) nervous system and the parasympathetic (relaxation response). When done over weeks and months, these body-based practices strengthen one's capacity to be steady and relaxed and located (grounded) in the body.

Practicing Ritual

Rituals can also strengthen us when we are intimidated. For example, the simple act of clearing space at a table and lighting a candle can focus your awareness and induce a feeling of comfort. Even the act of recording a dream in a dedicated dream journal can provide a feeling that a difficult dream is contained, held in place. Placing pictures around you of supportive people, spiritual guides, or mentors can fortify you with a feeling of connection to that which is kind, compassionate, and forgiving. Comforting music can be used to steady the nerves. These simple acts, best repeated daily, work when we infuse them with intention; that is, with a prayerful yearning for that which is Good and Loving to predominate.

Cultivating Compassion

A focus on compassion steadies us in the face of stress, especially if the threat is shame-based. Cultivating an attitude of loving-kindness towards oneself can be an antidote to the ill effects of a judgmental attitude, which, if allowed, will weaken us. Our connection to compassion can be strengthened through daily practices of sitting still, utilizing the calming breath, and remembering someone—a friend, loved one, or spiritual mentor—who embodies compassion.

I have found that a test of how compassionate I am can be done by looking at myself in the mirror. This simple, straightforward encounter with myself can tell me how comfortable or judgmental I am with myself on any given day. I recommend using the mirror as a daily practice to deepen your compassion. Simply linger in front of a mirror before you leave the bathroom and see how you feel towards yourself when you look into your eyes. You may not want to look. Consider why this would be? While noticing anything unpleasant or that you do not like about yourself, connect to a feeling of compassion or remember someone who embodies unconditional acceptance. The following practice of connecting with the source may help.

Connecting with the Source

There may be times when you cannot generate a feeling of love and safety. Concentrating on a loving source other than yourself may help steady you in the face of any feeling that would unnerve you. We humans often do this through a relationship with the Divine. At various times in my life, I have found the image of Christ, Buddha, Mother Mary, Quan Lin, and other spiritual presences helpful to connect me with a feeling of love and safety.

But just as importantly, I have also connected to the feeling of love by remembering someone human: my grandmother (through whom I first learned unconditional love), a best friend, or my mentor. In fact, for all of the emphasis on relaxation and meditation for stress relief in our culture, I find that simply remembering someone who loves me is the most reliable way to induce a feeling of safety. Even more, if I imagine breathing in this person's essence (their kindness and love) into my lungs, allowing their goodness to circulate to every cell of my body, I feel less alone. This is important because isolation is one of the biggest drivers of stress, feeling that "we are in it all by ourselves."

Spending time in Nature can recalibrate our nervous system and pull us out of a hyper-aroused fight or flight response. The power of the natural environment is too often overlooked in our modern sped-up culture, wherein we can spend days on end without ever being outside among trees, birds, lush vegetation, and flowing water.

Listening to Anxiety

We tend to think of intense and sustained anxiety as a disorder in our culture, the result of imbalanced neurochemistry in need of correcting through medication. My early training as a psychologist fostered this idea years ago. But I have increasingly moved away from a pathological disease orientation and found it more helpful to see anxiety as part of an elegant guidance system that alerts us to danger. Of course, the perceived danger can be external or internal. The unease of anxiety, for example, might be a warning of the impending danger of a demotion if you neglect to meet an upcoming deadline. In such a situation, the purpose of anxiety would be to help you do something to make yourself safer: asking for additional help to share the workload or renegotiating the deadline.

The anxiety, however, could just as well be the anticipation of a critical voice that might overtake you if you make any mistake on the project at hand. The solution for this would be to identify that judgmental voice and vocalize it. Speaking aloud a self-critical voice gets it out in the open and thus prevents it from operating in the background unnoticed. Some people might object to speaking a critical voice out loud, thinking that this would "give it more power." But I have found the opposite to be true. When you hear a critical voice spoken (by yourself), it usually makes the punitive nature of that voice more apparent and thus weakens its influence. Surprisingly, I have found that "speaking the negative voice" can do greater good than simply repeating positive affirmations in an attempt to suppress a critical voice inside.

If you become accustomed to turning inward and listening to your anxiety, rather than attempting to ignore or distract yourself from it, you are likely to develop an understanding of the danger to which it is alerting you. For example, is the anxiety warning you of a situation you should do something about in the external world? Or is the anxiety driven by negative, internal voices that need to be made explicit and then countered with compassion for yourself?

Often we simply focus on the discomfort of anxiety itself and do not probe the meaning of the disturbance and thus do not inquire of it as an intelligent warning system from Nature attempting to communicate something important.

When studying nightmares, we are often afraid of encountering feelings that would overwhelm us: shame, pain, and possible memories associated with the disturbing dream. We need, therefore, a steadying connection to love and safety so that we can drop down into the anxious feelings to discover just what it is that alarms us.

Finding Therapeutic Support

If your response to a frightening dream continues to be overwhelming, such that you cannot sit still to write or talk about it, then it can be helpful to find the support of a skillful psychotherapist who understands how to calm the nervous system—not just do talk therapy. I particularly like some of the newer body-based therapies like Somatic Experiencing (Levine, 2008) that help you engage in calming, consoling actions (like intentional breathing) while allowing for and describing a frightful feeling or memory.

It took me years before I admitted that I needed the guidance of a therapist. Like many, I had survived a difficult childhood by becoming hyperindependent. I had developed what I now see as a pseudo-independence (not deep autonomy) that protected me from exposing my vulnerability. Unfortunately, this strategy cut me off from needed empathy, comfort, and understanding from others. Finally, choosing a therapist was in some ways like a defeat for me, an admission that I could not solve the conundrums of my life alone. Discovering a skillful therapist (which required thoughtful searching) ended up being the Great Shortcut, a much quicker way of finding the wisdom I needed than I would have found on my own.

I recommend therapy with a caveat in mind. Not all therapists are created equal. You are fortunate if you find someone not only intelligent but also compassionate, someone not detached and emotionally uninvolved but instead genuinely cares for you and delights in knowing you. In addition to this, you will greatly benefit if you acquire a therapist who understands depth psychology and has done their own humbling investigation into themselves.

Increasing Tolerance for Discomfort

The purpose of establishing safety within yourself is to increase your tolerance for discomfort when you feel disturbed by something you have dreamed. By staying still long enough to calm yourself and study a difficult dream—and hopefully write a detailed description of it—you move from a position of avoidance to a posture of strength. The simple act of finally facing what has threatened you has far-reaching benefits, not only in stopping chronic nightmares but in working through other challenging situations of your life.

For some whose traumatic memories are recalled as a result of a nightmare, or who may be afraid that they will remember such if they become quiet, it may take great effort to sit still and find a steadying, pleasurable breath. The body may respond initially to the anticipated threat with increased heart rate, trembling, and faster breathing. Allowing these bodily responses without trying to push them away gives the nervous system time to discharge distress and eventually acclimate to the present moment.

If you wait long enough and tolerate discomfort, your nervous system will eventually begin to calm itself. Some people caught in panic forget this and attempt to rush away from distress, leading only to more anxiety. When we stay in the presence of a difficult emotion—breathing slightly fuller and slower than usual while consoling ourselves with reminders that we are safe in the here and now—anxiety *habituates*; that is, it gradually lessens. This is the result of an algorithm built into our emotional and physical bodies. There is an innate intelligence within us that can figure out what to do and bring us back to a feeling of safety if we do not turn away and patiently tolerate discomfort.

I remember a time in my life when I realized the truth of this.

The Chair That Became My Teacher

At the time, I was going through a sobering life review, a process that required me to tolerate many humbling realizations of mistakes and failures in the past. This is a common experience at midlife when you have accumulated enough evidence to realize that you need a major course correction if you are to be satisfied in the second half of your life. I knew the result of this endeavor would be greater wisdom, but facing my shortcomings was indeed challenging. Sometimes shame would sweep over me, causing despair. Other times anxiety would overtake me, and at first, I would not even know the reason for this. The apprehension I felt was intense: my body would become painfully stressed, so much so that I sometimes found it difficult to inhale fully.

It has now been so long ago that I scarcely recall the troubling situations I was reviewing, but what I do remember is how stormy the disturbing emotions were. They would sweep over me at the end of the day after work when I would be home alone, and because I wanted to understand their purpose (as opposed to distracting myself from them), I had no choice but to let myself drop fully into the stream of chaotic feelings that had been stirred.

At the time I had just purchased a large stuffed leather chair, and I could not have done so at a better moment. It became my home base, my safe place, for enduring the onslaught of troubling feelings—anxiety, grief, regret. I would crank the leg support up and lean back into a reclining position. The comfort of the thick, soft cushions helped me relax and surrender and thus allow my feelings to take me wherever they wanted.

I learned a great deal in this process. I discovered many insights that helped me make sense of patterns of thought and attitudes that had cheated me out of a full and satisfying life. I only came to these crucial realizations, however, as a result of enduring intense discomfort and trusting the downward pull into difficult emotions.

This experience lasted off and on for several months, and I was only able to endure the ordeal, a confrontation with the truth of myself, by finding comfort and safety in that oversized, loving recliner chair. It held and comforted me, and I was thus able to let go and surrender fully to a process that proved quite valuable.

The point of my story is that it is vital to be connected to a feeling of safety and comfort when encountering uncomfortable emotions, as happens when you study a nightmare. The more pleasure you can give the body, the better. I know some people who do this by wrapping themselves up in a comforting (sometimes weighted) blanket, snug and tight. Others do a few yoga poses. Whatever the means, it is important to establish the feeling of safety within yourself. From there, you can investigate a dream by following your deeper feelings which can lead to many useful insights.

2

Taking the
Crucial Step

A decisive moment in bringing an end to the suffering caused by nightmares is when someone stops, turns, and faces their disturbing dream. This is a major turning point like no other because it counters the entrenched, knee-jerk tendency to avoid and distance ourselves from the upsetting emotions evoked by a disturbing dream. The act of turning and facing a nightmare summons up courage and sets in motion healing forces within the personality.

I will now provide background on what led me to the above assertion. The pervasive attitude towards nightmares in our culture is that they serve no usefulness and are even harmful and disruptive, especially for someone already struggling with post-traumatic stress disorder (PTSD). For example, in the therapeutic community, it is known that nightmares are a distinguishing feature of PTSD and are often part of a prolonged hyper-vigilance response that leads to relationship distress, profound sleep disruption, and the many harmful health effects that flow from this: debilitating anxiety, depression, and even suicide. Nightmares may even be considered to be at the heart of what keeps PTSD from resolving itself. Given this, it is understandable how nightmare sufferers and health professionals alike simply wish to find a way to minimize or even eradicate terrifying dreams.

The attempt to do away with nightmares—without an investigation of how they might be helpful—is seen most clearly in the use of the prescription drug Prazosin. It is an alpha-blocker that was originally developed to treat high blood pressure but was incidentally discovered to also lessen nightmare frequency and intensity. Prazosin disrupts nightmares by lowering norepinephrine, a stress/arousal hormone, and thus decreases hyper-reactivity in dreaming. Yet, there are worrisome side effects, and nightmares return once the medication is discontinued. The underlying reasons for post-traumatic nightmares are not resolved.

Many people use alcohol and cannabis before bedtime to relax and, for some, to reduce nightmare frequency and intensity. Few realize, however, that these substances interrupt an essential stage of sleep, rapid eye movement (REM), where dreaming and the beneficial processes of memory consolidation, emotional regulation, and other advantageous functions occur. Nightmares may be lessened through alcohol and cannabis, but other problems may be inadvertently created as a result of interrupting the REM cycle. And as with Prazosin, once these substances are discontinued, there is a strong rebound effect, and nightmares return with even greater intensity.

An Updated Understanding of Disturbing Dreams

I propose that disruptive dreams give us an evolutionary advantage. They help us by bringing us face to face with patterns, attitudes, and behaviors that undermine us and rob us of our power and effectiveness in the world. My ideas follow an evolutionary perspective that asserts that we have developed certain functions to help us adapt to the ever-changing challenges of life on earth. I will summarize two theories about the purpose of disturbing dreams which led me to my current understanding.

As mentioned in the previous chapter, the *threat simulation hypothesis* of dreams by neuroscientist Antti Revonsuo (2000) proposes that we evolved the capacity to dream of threatening scenes to sharpen our protective instincts. By rehearsing responses to threats in our dreams, Revonsuo proposes, we are better equipped to employ these strategies in waking life. In one example, Revonsuo notes that children who live in proximity to war have far more disturbing dreams than do children who live in relative peace and safety, seemingly to hone their capacity to avoid danger. The severity and frequency of nightmares increase in response to real-life dangers.

I like Revonsuo's theory because it gives an understanding of the early evolutionary function of dreaming, which we likely share with other animals that dream. Dreaming evolved in us to simulate dangerous experiences and give us practice in basic survival skills. Through simulation, we learn more rapidly and without the tragic results of mistakes made that invariably come with the trial and error learning of waking life. However, as our brains have evolved, so have the functions of dreaming. I am proposing that stressful dreams do more than give us practice in avoiding external threats. In this book, I highlight the internal, *psychological* benefits of dreaming; that is, how dreaming can make us *wiser*, which I hold to be a primary purpose of nightmares for us humans. Disturbing dreams, even chronic nightmares associated with PTSD, are not simply the result of having been harmed. I propose that they are attempts by Nature to antidote the harmful effects of trauma and help us grow stronger.

Dr. Rosalind Cartwright (1996) at the University of Chicago studied the dreams of people who were depressed as a result of painful divorces. She noted that people who had conflictual dreams of their ex-partners over the previous year were far more likely to be free of depression than those who did not report such dreams. Interestingly, people who reported dreaming of their ex without experiencing *conflict* with them in their dreams did not show improvements in their depression. The same held true for depressed people in their study who did not report any dreams of their former spouse. This supports the idea that when we process disturbing emotions in our dreams, there is a beneficial effect in waking life.

Cartwright's research demonstrates that dreaming serves a crucial function by helping us diffuse difficult emotions like anxiety and depression. Our capacity to dream, and even dream intensely and disruptively, is how we process stressful events and feelings. In fact, most people who suffer a traumatic event adjust to and metabolize trauma in the weeks and months following a shocking situation. Disturbing dreams may initially contain images of the traumatic experience, but in most cases, these images disappear over time.

Sometimes, however, a person cannot absorb and integrate traumatic events like divorce, war, accidents, sexual abuse, and violence, and disturbing dreams may continue long afterward, as happens in PTSD. Dreaming itself may then become a primary source of distress. This occurs if the strength of the trauma is beyond the person's ability to process it. However, what if nightmares, even still, are attempting to help the sufferer?

I believe that disruptive dreams may continue long after a traumatizing event because of a grave danger to which all traumatized persons are vulnerable. The defensive strategies of fight, flight, and freeze that enable us to cope during a threatening event may be employed beyond the time they were helpful. While highly advantageous during a life and death crisis, the prolonged use of these emergency strategies can dramatically complicate and restrict a person's life. An example of this comes from a man I once knew who had fought in Vietnam.

We initially met in college, and being a few years older than I, I looked up to him for his discipline in academics, exercise, and the pristine way he ordered his dorm room and dress (starched, ironed shirts in those days). Compared to the rest of us just away from home for the first time, he carried the charisma of being an adult man, though only older than most of us by three years. I did not know that while I had been enjoying a carefree life in high school, he had already joined the Army and was fighting in the jungles of Vietnam. However, in the three years we knew one another in college, he never spoke of this despite our considering one another to be best of friends.

We were rarely in contact after college, but he called unexpectedly late one night some twenty years after we had last seen one another. I could tell that he had been drinking. With slurred speech, he opened the conversation starkly. "I'm haunted by my demons," he confessed. I had no idea what he meant until he related a recent incident. He said that he rarely went out to socialize anymore but had ventured out on a new date to see a movie. "I made sure that it had nothing to do with Nam (his first mention of war)," he said. "There I was, holding hands, eating popcorn, and the last thing I remember was seeing a police chase scene with the sound of churning blades of a low-flying helicopter. The next thing I know, people are screaming at me, and I realize that I'm crawling under their seats, trying to escape. I'm back in Nam." Embarrassed and shocked, he told me that this was why he had become socially isolated and compulsively worked all the time.

The High Cost of Continued Avoidance

We are hardwired to protect ourselves in the face of threatening events by employing fight, flight, or freeze strategies. Fighting, of course, is intended to overcome and neutralize an aggressor, while flight enables us to escape. If neither of these options is deemed feasible, then freeze may occur. Freezing may signal a lack of threat to an aggressor or make us less appealing to a predator. Freezing may also lessen psychological or physical pain by enabling us to "leave our bodies," dissociating so that we do not feel overwhelming emotional or physical distress.

While these three responses are highly advantageous, helping us avoid pain, injury, or death, these same protective strategies can also become harmful if utilized beyond their intended purpose. When engaged too long, these emergency strategies may undermine our ability to respond with precision and effectiveness to present-day challenges.

If an emergency strategy designed for a distressing event of the past is still active, as it was for my friend from college, we are in danger of misperceiving the details of the present moment. We may thus impose inaccurate and drastic measures that further complicate a present-day problem. We may over-react with aggression or use avoidance and become passive when we should speak up for ourselves. This state of chronic reactivity has vast disadvantages. Hair-trigger anger and irritability may unexpectedly overtake us and create harm in relationships. Or in the opposite extreme, we may become overly passive when we should be assertive and advocate for what we need.

When a part of us remains in a state of chronic hyper-arousal—being ever-vigilant to avoid a repeat of past threatening or painful events—there are enormous limitations to both our effectiveness and fulfillment in work, play, and love. Intrusive memories can prevent us from being fully present and undermine our ability to concentrate at work or enjoy a loving moment with our partners. We may inaccurately suspect hostile intentions from a co-worker whose personality or physical stature is reminiscent of someone who once harmed us. This same dynamic can be observed in the animal world when an adopted dog abused by a tall, bearded male, for example, is forever fearful and reactive to men with these same characteristics. When our earlier defensive strategies to avoid pain remain active beyond their original usefulness, our freedom to explore and live life fully may be dramatically curtailed.

Another prolonged response to trauma may be a chronic state of under-arousal (think of the freeze response) that can manifest as depression, fatigue, listlessness, and pervasive meaninglessness. Someone can be responsible, perform adequately at work, and even keep their home in good order, but they lack the fulfillment of being fully engaged in the world.

Again, the opposite may be true: someone may silently suffer from chronic hyper-vigilance whereby they can never relax and consequently live in a narrow range of emotions, anxiety being the predominant feeling experienced. As a result, an underlying dread may be the primary emotional state that is felt, crowding out other emotions such as playfulness, sensuality, curiosity, and joy.

Someone suffering nightmares long after a traumatic event may resort to exhausting personal rituals and tactics to avoid frightening dreams and the memory of a trauma. They may avoid sleep until the wee hours of the night. Bedroom doors may be triple bolted and secured with heavy furniture to give someone the semblance of safety when waking out of an intruder dream, still unable to distinguish what is real from what is imagined. In addition to chronic sleep loss and pervasive anxiety, perhaps the most pernicious effect for nightmare sufferers is the deterioration of trust in themselves. It is easy for one to assume that something is terribly wrong or broken with their minds, or they may secretly wonder if they are crazy or going mad. Self-doubt is accentuated all the more due to believing that one is helpless, that nothing can be done to stop the dreaded dreams, simply because they occur during sleep when one has no control over what happens.

Thus, chronic avoidance and hyper-sensitivity to situations or people that trigger us exact an enormous toll. Not only do we miss out on experiencing the fullness of life, but we are also in a dangerous situation from an evolutionary perspective—we are vulnerable to misreading people or situations and thus may miscalculate the kind of response that is required.

It is here that nightmares come to our aid. In my view, disturbing dreams bring us face to face with threatening people, places, and things to provide us with rehearsals for developing mastery in responding to threats. It seems to me that there is an intelligence in the dreaming process that pushes us to move beyond the highly reactive responses of fighting, fleeing, or freezing, since these emergency strategies can endanger us if engaged too long.. However, while I suspect that dreaming evolved initially to help us be more prepared for physical dangers in waking life, I imagine that the dream's agenda is far more complex than this today.

The threats in modern life more often come to us from within ourselves. As someone trained in depth psychology, I observe that the characters in our dreams are often symbolic of forces in the personality, attitudes within us that may hurt or help us. Nightmares, for example, may confront someone with a life-threatening addiction or suicidal depression. However, at a more subtle level, dreams may reveal internalized self-defeating criticism that may thwart our best efforts at success. Dreams may also show psychological deficits, having not developed needed strengths earlier in life, and we thus may be brought face to face with potentials we have disavowed (think of the nightmare of my warriors). Just as often, we may have to suffer humbling realizations in dreams that threaten our idealized and unrealistic self-image, but which, if absorbed, can help us be more balanced and relate to the world realistically.

However, regardless of whether you find dream figures to be metaphors for aspects of yourself or not, the mere act of turning and facing that which is threatening, either while in your dream or when reviewing it once awake, establishes your *authority*. As you will learn in the next section, this has enormous ramifications in dreaming. In most cases, this bold and decisive act stops nightmares or at least lessens their intensity. For this reason, I call the switch from avoidance to proactively facing and investigating threatening dreams *The Crucial Step*.

I propose that Nature seeks to elicit a creative response from us to move us beyond over-reactive aggression and avoidance so that we face forces within ourselves with self-awareness. For some readers, it will seem that I am now overstating the case. Is Nature actually "intending" to elicit creative responses from us? Or am I being anthropomorphic and projecting consciousness and motivations onto the dreaming process that are not inherently there? Let's explore this in the following discussion about an innovative method for intervening in chronic nightmares.

The Surprising Benefits of Turning and Facing

As evidence for my assertion that Nature seeks to elicit a proactive, creative response from us through nightmares, consider the unexpected results of a surprisingly simple treatment for nightmare sufferers that I briefly mentioned in the previous chapter: Image Rehearsal Therapy (IRT).

Researchers at the University of New Mexico School of Medicine and the Sleep and Human Health Institute in Albuquerque (Krakow and Zadra, 2010) discovered that the majority of nightmare sufferers who completed a six-hour IRT program conducted over three weeks dramatically reduced the frequency of their nightmares. Not only that, participants reported less anxiety, depression, and symptoms of PTSD. The brief training consisted of learning basic relaxation skills, and then rewriting the narrative to have a different outcome. For those who completed the training and continued to rehearse their revised dream for 2-4 weeks, 90% of participants reported a dramatic (not just statistically significant) reduction in nightmare frequency.

This study is noteworthy because participants were given open-ended instruction to create a revised version of their nightmare in any way they wished. They were not directed in what to include in the revision, but instead, they were asked to create an alternative narrative that was different (and presumably less anxiety-provoking) than the original, frightening dream. Note the proactive response that was encouraged.

A few years later, researchers at the University of Tulsa (Davis, 2008) wanted to determine how effective Image Rehearsal Therapy would be for those having suffered trauma. Everyone in the study met the criteria for a PTSD diagnosis. The average number of nightmares for people in this study before treatment was 4.4 each week, with an average intensity level of 2.96 on a scale of 1-4. The average amount of sleep per night was 5.5 hours before treatment, and one-third of the participants reported needing more than an hour to fall asleep each night—clearly, a sleep-deprived group.

Participants were taught basic relaxation skills, then directed to choose their worst dream (unlike the earlier studies in New Mexico) and describe it in written form. They were then asked to create a revised version. The results of this study involving 49 people were quite positive. When assessing the effects of treatment, either three or six months later, 89% of those graduating from the program reported having no nightmares in the previous week, and 79% reported having no memory of having had a nightmare in the previous month. Not only this, the study did not rely on self-reporting methods alone but assessed physical reactivity to audio-recorded descriptions of their nightmares by measuring stress responses throughout the body, including facial muscles—a means of detecting subtle distress. For those who completed the treatment, their physiological arousal was "nearly abolished" when re-exposed to descriptions of their nightmares.

What We Can Learn

I wish to make three points about the above studies. One, despite the remarkable results from a treatment that is relatively simple and brief (though not necessarily easy for some nightmare sufferers), few therapists, including those offering treatments to veterans, know of this potent intervention. Unfortunately, because of this, nightmares may be ignored entirely or at least not addressed directly, given that many therapists feel inadequate, for lack of training, to deal with distressing dreams. On the other hand, some therapists may spend an exorbitant amount of time focused on interpreting a disturbing dream without helping a client mobilize their resources to assert their authority and thus become proactive and craft a better ending, which in itself can likely bring an end to recurrent nightmares. Many nightmare sufferers could be helped if more therapists learned of Image Rehearsal Therapy.

Secondly, a most interesting finding from these studies is that participants benefited in ways other than reducing the frequency of troubling dreams. Two of the classic symptoms of PTSD—anxiety and depression—improved, as did the quality of sleep. In other words, it appears that one effective way to treat PTSD is to empower people to deal with their nightmares, rather than assuming, as many do, that nightmares are the result of PTSD and that improvements in dream quality can only be made by first addressing the trauma itself. Giving someone the skills to turn, face, and creatively respond to nightmare imagery may very well be a valuable way of treating PTSD.

Lastly, these studies demonstrate how quickly nightmare distress can be reduced when someone takes just four steps: One, utilizing relaxation skills, which I refer to as Establishing Safety Within. Two, facing the nightmare directly by recording the dream narrative in written form.[2] Three, making a creative response by rewriting a dream with a more positive outcome, and fourthly, rehearsing the new dream narrative in the days and weeks afterward.

Note that these studies did not attempt to interpret dreams. In fact, they carefully avoided doing so and did not even prescribe how a dream could or should be rewritten. Nor did the studies focus on other aspects of PTSD or intentionally address a traumatic event. Yet remarkable results ensued. For this reason, I suspect that one of the fundamental purposes of nightmares, especially for those suffering PTSD, is to elicit a

---

2. Some versions of IRT omit this step.

proactive, creative response and thus move someone beyond their entrenched patterns of avoidance and reactivity. When a person takes what I call The Crucial Step and faces what they have avoided, they establish *agency* and thus activate resources essential to human survival and success: *creativity* and *courage*. I cannot emphasize enough just how beneficial this one act is.

Contrary Interpretations

There are admittedly other ways of interpreting the positive results from Image Rehearsal Therapy. I will review two which are in opposition to what I am proposing.

Krakow and Zadra (2006), long-time practitioners and educators on the use of IRT, attribute the therapeutic outcome of IRT to correcting a "damaged imagery system." Using a metaphor from computer science, they assert that the "patient's dysfunctional imagery system" is akin to "corrupted software (p. 62)." The antidote to this dire condition can be found by the "reactivation" of the proper use of imagery, meaning that nightmare sufferers can be educated to use their imagination in purposeful, positive ways, which involves rewriting a distressing dream to have a better outcome.

Chronic, recurrent disturbing dreams are viewed to be the result of something having become dysfunctional within the personality or brain, a mistake of an individual, or perhaps Nature itself. However, this situation can be remediated through education and the proper use of imagination (when rescripting a disturbing dream).

Many people I have spoken with who have studied their disturbing dreams and found useful insights, even life-changing wisdom, will find the above explanation to be pessimistic and narrowly based on a pathological disease model and misreads what Nature is attempting to accomplish through the dreaming process. Like the pain-sensing intelligence of the body, nightmares might just as well be seen as an elegant signaling process that warns the dreamer of danger. The fact that physical pain or emotional disturbance from a dream is difficult need not necessarily mean that either is bad for us. In fact, it can be argued that the painful disturbance is precisely what causes us to attend to something injurious. More on this later.

To the credit of the IRT theorists, imagination has been shown to be a potent force for intervening in nightmares. Imagining an alternative narrative to a disturbing dream can potentially antidote years of suffering. For those who might be suspicious that the use of the imagination is "just fantasy," I refer them to Joe Dispenza's (2014) book, You Are the Placebo, which is an inspiring collection of stories of people who have harnessed the power of imagination to heal grave physical illnesses.

Another explanation for why we suffer nightmares and why they can be changed through IRT comes from Revonsuo (2000). As previously discussed, he views threatening dreams as simulations by Nature to hone our instincts for survival. While this explanation seems plausible to me, especially when considering why we initially evolved the ability to dream, I have wondered, "Why would someone continue to dream of past trauma when the threat is no longer present in waking life?" For example, why would a soldier continue to have nightmares of a battle scene in Vietnam decades after having lived without war in a safe, rural community in North America?

When I posed this question to Revonsuo (personal communication, Nov. 30, 2021), he suggested that the mechanism that creates dreams uses the most distressing memories to orchestrate simulations. If there is still a highly negative emotional charge associated with a traumatic memory, then the dream will continue to build simulations on this, as if the person is still in danger. In other words, the dreaming mechanism does not realize the person is no longer in danger in waking life. "The dream production mechanism searches in long-term episodic memory" for memories "that have the highest negative charge (representing the worst threat one has ever encountered), and because the traumatic event is so much more highly negatively charged than anything else, the system always finds the same memories to base the simulation on." In Revonsuo's view, the dream simulation mechanism "gets stuck on rehearsing and simulating (a traumatic memory) over and over again. The system is in that sense 'stupid' and cannot evaluate whether it makes sense to rehearse it any longer (A. Revonsuo, personal communication,

Nov. 30, 2021)." (See the footnote[3] below describing Revonsuo's theory of why IRT works.)

Here again, my understanding of disturbing dreams does not see nightmares as resulting from a flawed system, but rather dreams are intelligent simulations to encourage mastery. If someone is still in a reactive, defensive, and especially victimized relationship to past trauma, in my view, dreaming intelligence presses the person to adapt by adopting a proactive and creative posture in how they deal with the threat.

At this point, I am not certain how any of the theories discussed here could be proven, my own included, given the limitations of our current tools of scientific investigation. As mentioned above, it may be that each theorist is seeing just one aspect of the elephant. However, in the absence of any definitive and agreed-upon theory of what causes nightmares, I find that a view of dreams as benevolent, intentional, and intelligent rather than flawed certainly provides more motivation for a nightmare sufferer to study a frightful dream, which, of course, is already a difficult task.

The Ritual of Turning and Facing

Understandably, it can be a formidable task to record a dream in detail which we would rather forget. This is particularly true for someone who suffers frequent disturbing dreams which disrupt sleep and undermine faith in themselves. Nightmare sufferers often feel persecuted by their dreams, leading them to feel that they are being attacked by hostile forces intent on their harm. Others may take disturbing dreams as evidence that they are deeply disturbed, sick, or in the case of trauma, damaged beyond help.

An antidote to such despair can be found in making a basic presumption about the purpose of dreaming. When dreams are understood as Nature's attempt to help us and are part of an intelligent process designed to grow wisdom in us, one can trust the difficult process of facing a disturbing

---

3. "Why image rehearsal theory works, I speculate that it lowers the negative emotional charge of those memories and thus releases the dream production system to search also elsewhere in memory for other topics to base its dream simulations on (A. Revonsuo, personal communication, Nov. 30, 2021)."

dream. With this in mind, I recommend remembering the following two questions when tempted to turn away from a difficult dream.

1. **Is this dream for or against me?** This question helps to crystalize any misgivings we harbor about the dreaming process. Admittedly, someone who has suffered hellish nightmares, especially if related to trauma, will find it challenging to genuinely feel that there is anything of value to disruptive dreams. Even after studying my dreams for over thirty years, I sometimes feel that there is "something bad" about a disturbing dream upon awakening. Despite my training, I am prone to forget, at least initially, that difficult dreams are intended to help me. Therefore, I remind myself, "Oh, as hard as this dream is to approach, there's something of value in it for me." This simple switch from suspiciousness to having faith in the dreaming process gives me the courage to study a dream and find value from it.

2. **Am I approaching my dreams with respect?** I can think of nothing more valuable to enhance the study of your dreams than recording them in a journal. I love Carl Jung's (2009) advice in *The Red Book* about the importance of recording dreams in a special place and way.

> I should advise you to put it all down as beautifully as you can in some beautifully bound book... Then when these things are in some precious book, you can go to the book and turn over the pages, and for you, it will be your church—your cathedral—the silent places of your spirit where you will find renewal. If anyone tells you that it is morbid or neurotic and you listen to them— then you will lose your soul—for in that book is your soul.

I sometimes arrange a table with flowers and candles before studying a dream. The picture below gives an example of how I used ribbons to create a boundary, sometimes known as a sacred circle, a designated place where one can be safe and access wisdom.

Giving this kind of attention to dreams creates *containment*, a psychological holding vessel in which the mysterious process of creativity and change can occur. A dream journal can also serve this same function, especially with nightmares, because the disturbance can be held in a safe place.

Beyond the Crucial Step

Once you have established a feeling of safety within yourself and then recorded a dream in detail, the third step is to make a creative response, which is at the heart of what brings a nightmare to completion. While there are no limits in how someone can respond creatively to a dream, I find that they are typically five categories of the creative response.

- Moving from Actor to Director.
- Absorbing Difficult Truth.
- Exposing Undermining Influences.
- Knowing Your Adversary.
- Advocating for the Helpless.

Each one of these responses is described in the following chapters.

Making the Creative Response

This third step in the Nightmare Completion process is the most complex and allows your creative impulses to flourish. The following five chapters give an overview of what is possible when making a response to a nightmare, but they are by no means the only ones possible. You are only limited by your imagination.

Any of the creative responses listed below can dramatically change your experience of a dream. Whereas you are likely to feel initially frightened and filled with dread by a disturbing dream, the actions discussed here can lead you to feel gratitude and even awe for the intelligence that is at work in the dreaming process.

I have observed that most people do one of the following when they complete a nightmare.

- Moving from Actor to Director
- Absorbing Difficult Truth
- Knowing Your Adversary
- Realizing Undermining Influences
- Advocating for the Helpless

Holding these five possibilities in mind can guide you when determining what the best response is for you to complete a nightmare.

Moving from Actor to Director

The heart of Nightmare Completion is creativity. It involves studying how you acted in the dream and then imagining how you might behave differently. Creating a second version of your dream allows you to rehearse a more courageous and skillful way of acting under threat so that the dream's outcome is more satisfying, leaving you empowered rather than victimized. Though revising a dream this way may seem "just made up" and "pretend," when done with sincerity and genuine feelings, this simple process can have enormous benefits.

The change from being a reactive participant to a creative agent in your dream is similar to switching from being an actor to a director. An actor behaves according to an assigned role, whereas a director has the power to rewrite scenes, introduce new characters, and make the narrative go in a new direction than what was originally scripted. In psychology, such a change from living out a role that others have prescribed for you to becoming someone who originates their own ideas and behaviors is referred to as having *agency*, the ability to determine the course of your own life.

The idea that we can change our dreams is novel for most people and may strike them as unrealistic. After all, we are asleep when we dream and usually are not even aware until later that we have been dreaming. Additionally, most people assume that once a dream is over, nothing more can be done.

However, there is a way of re-entering the memory of a dream to become an active participant. I am not talking about lucid dreaming, a technique of becoming aware that you are dreaming while you are still asleep. No, I am referring to going back into the memory of a dream once awake. In contrast to lucid dreaming, you do not have to wait until you have another dream and become lucid (aware that you are dreaming) before creating a different ending. Instead, you can re-enter the memory of your dream immediately at will or choose to review it hours or days later and then rewrite your dream with a different narrative that feels satisfying and relieving.

The Woman Who Got Caught by Her Ankle

When I first started listening to the dreams of my clients, I had few ideas about how to deal with them. More often than not, I was stupefied when someone told me a dream. I had no idea what to do. Previous to working with my therapist, I thought that if I were smart enough, I would be able to immediately provide an interpretation that would help a client. I have since realized how unrealistic this expectation was and how disadvantageous this can be to a client.

Fortunately, through my therapist's example, I learned how dreams could be explored innocently without imposing predetermined explanations on them. By interacting with dream figures once awake, much more information can be discovered than what was in the original dream. The additional knowledge, more often than not, provides crucial insights into the purpose of a dream.

With this approach in mind, I helped a woman re-enter the memory of a disturbing dream, one that was typical of many nightmares she had had in the previous year. We picked up right where her dream had ended, and we both were quite surprised by what we found.

At the time of the dream, Jill had left her boyfriend with whom she had lived for a year. Feeling "suffocated," she had moved to another city, and she did so without telling him beforehand. Despite creating a safe distance, Jill dreamed repeatedly of her ex chasing her. Each time she would wake up in a panic.

When Jill told me her latest chase dream, I did not want to presume that it was merely symbolic. I first wished to determine if she felt herself to be in any danger. "No, not really," she said, showing no concern. "He's not that kind of guy. He would never hurt me." I pressed further, "Is there a danger that he would stalk you, show up unannounced?" Again, "No, if he wanted to track me down, it would be easy for him to find me. I'm back in my hometown. But that's not his style."

I asked, "Why do you think he pursues you in your dreams?" Clueless, Jill was as dumbfounded as when waking from her nightmares.

I asked Jill to re-enter her dream as if she was experiencing it for the first time and describe in detail what happens. Closing her eyes, she took several long breaths and recounted the dream.

> I'm running up a mountainous ravine strewn with rocks, and I look back over my shoulder and see my boyfriend behind at a distance. He's chasing me, and I panic and run faster, but the more I try to outdistance him, the quicker he gains speed on me.

Jill opened her eyes and stared at me for help. I had no idea about the dream's purpose or significance, which is typical of me even today when I first hear someone's dream. In fact, I have come to value such an open-minded attitude because it frees me from prematurely imposing interpretations on the dream that were not intended. I often say to myself, "I have no idea what this dream means, so let me listen and discover what it wants to tell me," an approach that I gleaned from the writings of Carl Jung. (1989, p. 170).

I invited Jill to explore the dream further. "Given that you are safe here," I assured her, "could you go back to where the dream ended and see if anything else wants to happen?"

Jill closed her eyes again, took a few relaxing breaths, and re-entered her inner world.

> I'm running with all my might, almost out of breath. But suddenly, I trip and fall. He's right behind me. But…(Jill pauses). Wow…

Jill's waking imagination inserted unexpected action.

> When I fall, he trips as well.

"And?" I encouraged her.

> I hurry to my feet, but as I'm about to get away, he grabs my ankle and stops my escape.

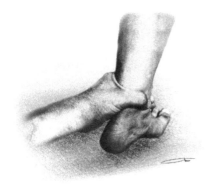

Jill opened her eyes, surprised, again wondering what to do.

"Does the dream feel complete? Is it over?" I asked. She immediately shakes her head, "No."

Still, having no idea where this exploration was going, I asked, "Could we return once more to the drama, but this time add a question? Why not turn around and face the man and ask why he's after you?"

Contrary to how Jill usually behaved in her dream, she now felt safe enough to do what she had never done. Closing her eyes, she re-entered her dream and allowed the drama to unfold further. After only a few seconds of silence, she jolted me by shouting out loud, demanding an answer.

Why have you been chasing me?!

My body was startled at the force of Jill's demand. Clearly, she was treating her dream figure as someone real, not fantasy. Consequently, she had an emotional response to him, which I have observed yields greater results in dreamwork than dispassionate analysis.

We both waited in silence for Jill's imagination to provide more information. I encouraged her, "Listen for what he wants to say." To Jill's surprise, the man answered, and she spoke his words with force.

To stop you from running from yourself!

Jill opened her eyes widely, surprised as I was by the declaration. "He would never say something like that," she assured me. "He wouldn't even think of it," she said with sarcasm. It appeared that the man chasing her was not the same as the one she had left in waking life, a phenomenon I have observed countless times when someone allows a dream figure to speak. While the dream figure looked the same, he gave an entirely uncharacteristic answer. I have noticed this to be the case often. Though a person you dream of may look exactly like someone you know in waking life, do not assume they are the same. Allow them to act of their own accord when you interact with them in your imagination.

As Jill pondered her boyfriend's pointed challenge, she became more transparent than I had ever witnessed her be. She described having lost most of her friends over the years because of not working through difficulties in relationships. "It's true," she admitted, "I run, really before there's a confrontation. If I see a friendship headed towards conflict, I just disappear and never look back."

"What troubles you about conflict?" I asked. Jill paused, "Hmm...," as if considering the question for the first time. "It's my anger that scares me," she admitted.

"Why would you be afraid of that?" I asked.

I learned how Jill had disavowed her anger while growing up in a well-behaved family that did not tolerate discord. At the heart of her problem was her troublesome relationship with her father. While he was mild-mannered and never raised his voice, her father would persist in an argument and never give in. Jill came to resent and avoid his lectures and political rants, for she knew that if she challenged him, she would be caught in an endless barrage of arguments until she backed down. Once she left home, Jill continued suppressing her anger, and thus never learned to skillfully voice her protest. Consequently, she feared that if she dared speak up, which she had done a few disastrous times, her rage would spew out of her uncontrollably and damage the tentative friendships she had formed.

Jill's bitterness could not be completely hidden, however. In telling me more of her story, I better understood her dry, sarcastic humor, which invariably would leave me feeling uneasy and never able to laugh. Even though she told me that she "hated being angry," irritableness lived in the background of her seemingly playful sarcasm. And while people did not tell her, I was sure that it made those around her feel uncomfortable, causing them to keep their distance.

The chase dream gave Jill valuable insight into her avoidant behavior that had caused her isolation and loneliness. Even with this valuable information, however, it seemed to me that the dream was not complete. I asked, "What do you want to do now, given that you realize the truth of what your dream has told you?" Uncertain, Jill mused in silence, again letting her imagination take the lead.

> I see myself standing up and saying to him, 'You're right. I do run.
> It's a bad habit of mine.'

And that is how Jill left the dream. She had nothing more to say. However, our discussion did not end there. In the following weeks, we role-played how she could approach people with whom she had a conflict. With practice, Jill saw how she could be true to herself, speaking with directness and honesty, without being argumentative and controlling as her father had been. Of course, all of this was possible because she had re-entered her dream as an active participant, proactively posing questions and listening for responses from her dream figure, thus gaining unexpected insight.

This method of re-entering dreams and creating conversations with dream figures builds on the work of Carl Jung, who developed an investigative approach to dreams called Active Imagination. In another book of mine, *Your Dream's Ten Best Friends* (2022), I refer to this method as *Let Dream Presences Speak*. Entering into imagical dialogue with dream figures is a way to allow the dream, the creative imagination, to continue in a waking state. This is a form of play that most all of us did in our early years. Children enjoy a rich fantasy life, speaking with stuffed animals, super-hero figures, or invisible imaginary friends. While this method may seem contrived for adults, it is actually a way to make contact with dormant sides of yourself that have been pushed to the background of your personality.

When Jill spoke with the former boyfriend of her dream, she was not, of course, speaking with him. She recognized that her ex would never say to her what her dream figure said. Jill was thus accessing a wiser part of herself that could help her make better decisions in life because of the self-honesty involved.

Entering into conversations with dream figures is one way to re-enter a dream, again, once awake, and revise a dream. There are, of course, countless ways to reimagine a nightmare. In Image Rehearsal Therapy, reviewed in the previous chapter, *Taking the Crucial Step*, directions on how to re-write a dream are intentionally open-ended. "Change the dream in any way you like" would be the advice for re-writing nightmares.

While I believe it is advantageous for dreamers to craft their unique responses when re-writing nightmares, rather than following one imposed on them by someone else, I have found a few guiding principles that make some creative responses more potent than others. Before I describe these principles, let me give a reminder about the reason for them.

I believe that one of the primary purposes of nightmares is to orchestrate simulation scenarios, similar to flight simulations used to train pilots. When we review our nightmares and observe how we acted, we can become aware of our blind spots, ways in which we are weak or overreactive, and thus ineffective. By reimagining a dream, we train ourselves to be more effective by moving beyond rigid, highly reactive behaviors, which only exacerbate problems. Furthermore, Nature appears to place great value on us not remaining stuck in emergency strategies like fight, flight, or freeze, which restrict and complicate our lives if still utilized well after a stressful event. By orchestrating challenging events, nightmares push us to adopt more nuanced and skillful responses to intimidating, threatening situations.

When you consider making a creative response to a disturbing dream, I recommend that you bear these suggestions in mind.

- Solve the problem. Don't create more problems by being over-reactive or avoidant.
- Let unexpected solutions come to you.
- Favor solutions that also work in waking life.
- Choose solutions that have the least amount of collateral damage.
- Stay genuine. Follow actions that are true to your deeper feelings.
- Experiment with a new role. Try stepping out of your usual way of behaving.

Facing Criticism

The following story shows how one woman used the creative response of standing her ground to rewrite a nightmare. In the original version of her dream, Robin had fled in panic to escape a large group of people who had abused and demeaned her throughout her life.

> I am frantically stuffing my clothes into my suitcase, hoping that I will not be noticed when I leave. But as I emerge from my room, I encounter a host of people from my past waiting for me. They

immediately jeer and shame me for moving away. One of these is my former husband, who cruelly abused me throughout my marriage. Another is my mother, who both belittled and physically abused me throughout my childhood. Added to these are members of my church community, who acted as a cult, hyper-critical if you departed from the strict norms they fanatically held. There are also kids from my childhood: teens, girls who had derided me.

I wake up in a panic.

Robin, now in her mid-forties, had recently moved from her hometown, where she had known those in her dream. She had fallen in love with a man she trusted and with whom she wanted to start a new life. But at the time of the move, not one of her current friends (not those in the dream) supported her for making what they thought would turn out to be an impulsive and foolish mistake. Robin went against critical opinion despite her usually accommodating mode, trusted her heart, and relocated to another city.

The dream came several months after the move. It epitomized the collective judgment of Robin's family and religious community under which she had suffered for many years. She was thus shaken by the dream, as if her past had found its way into her new life.

I had recently introduced Robin to the essentials of nightmare completion. In working with her, I encouraged her first to find her calming breath and then re-enter the memory of her dream, adding, "If you could respond differently to the derisive people, what would you do?"

Robin immediately said, "I would say, 'Steady yourself. Don't run and see what happens.'"

Robin waited to see what her imagination would do if she held steady and did not flee. To her surprise, she felt an impulse to approach each spiteful person one by one, look into their eyes, not budging, and stay mindful of her calming breath. Robin had recently learned a loving-kindness meditation, so she drew upon the feeling of compassion for herself while she allowed (and tolerated) each person criticizing her.

This time Robin did not turn away, and in fact, even imagined speaking up on her behalf to some of the dream figures. With others, she simply breathed calmly and reminded herself of her basic goodness, all the while looking each critical person in the eyes and waiting until each one had nothing more to say. Immediately, Robin felt empowered.

Now let us consider what else she might have done that would likely have not been as effective. She might have been highly aggressive (gone into the fight response) and imagined having a gun with her and killing the

 large group of people who had been mean and critical of her over the years. (Not a solution with the least amount of collateral damage.) Another response might have been for her to go up to each person and slap their faces in reproof for having treated

her so badly. Obviously, this response would not be useful in waking life. Furthermore, would her aggression have freed her from caring so much about what others thought? Likely not.

I should insert here that there are situations when such extremely aggressive actions might very well be helpful to someone who has never felt the power of their protective anger. The imagination can provide a safe place to experiment with protective forces in the personality that may have been off-limits earlier in life. For example, some people learned to suppress any expression of anger, lest an abuser cause them more harm.

I was impressed with Robin's response because she connected with dignity in herself and consequently did not have to argue anyone out of their criticism. She remained settled and undaunted. As a result, she drained her tormentors of their negative power.

It should be noted that the way Robin behaved in the revised version of her dream was highly out of the ordinary for her. Usually, she would be unsettled, even unnerved, when criticized. Her creative response in her revised version was thus novel and out of character. She thus stepped into a new role, departing from her usual flight response.

I am not suggesting that you should never fight in self-defense when rewriting a dream. As mentioned above, for someone who typically freezes when threatened, fighting back in some form or another might be highly advantageous when revising a nightmare. However, I am advising that some responses have more power than others. Therefore imagine how a wiser, more potent version of yourself would act.

Taking the Creative Response a Step Further

Though Robin was satisfied with her new role in her revised dream, she was still curious if more wisdom might be available from the dream. So, I helped her explore the dream further by asking, "How might the critical voices of those in your dream be symbolic of forces that live within you?" (This is a method of dream investigation in which you consider that the various dream figures are symbolic of attitudes and behaviors within your personality.) Immediately Robin knew. She confessed to constantly second-guessing herself and not speaking up when she was in conflict with a friend or colleague. In other words, she was plagued by intimidating inner voices that robbed her of confidence. Being overly critical of herself was an earlier defensive strategy in her youth that had once made her safe—she learned to acquiesce to avoid harm from abusers in her family. This pattern no longer served her.

Robin was in danger of undermining her strengths and talents if she continued to run from criticism in her work relations and friendships. The dream deftly displayed her vulnerability and crafted a drama that showed how she was still living out an old and ineffective version of herself. Fortunately, Robin did not leave the dream where it ended. By re-entering the memory of the dream and creatively responding to the criticism hurled at her, she became more mindful of the inner criticisms that silently plagued her in everyday life.

You will note in the above example that Robin went beyond traditional Image Rehearsal Therapy. She not only crafted a different response to her critics when she revised her dream, but she then did interpretive work, seeing the hostile people in her dream as symbolic of her own self-criticism.

From Destruction to a New Life

When you imagine yourself as director of a dream, you can add dream figures that can help you. You can create a dialogue with people in your dream to understand them better. You can also assert yourself rather than remain frozen and passive. Essentially you can do anything that changes the dream from a tragic story to a drama that demonstrates your ability to solve challenging problems.

Another story shows how a man stopped chronic nightmares by taking an active role in his revised dream. Edward came to me because he repeatedly woke up in a panic when dreaming of his house burning down. The dreams were almost a virtual replay of an actual fire that had consumed his entire house. Here is one of the dreams that was typical of many that he suffered.

> I'm standing on my front lawn, still in bare feet beside my wife, shocked and still in disbelief that our house is going up in flames.

We watch in horror just as we did a few years ago when our home of thirty years disappeared before our eyes.

By the time of this dream, it had been several years since the fire, yet Edward continued to re-experience the tragedy repeatedly in his nightmares. After learning how to do Nightmare Completion, he rewrote his dream twice. In the first revision, he chose to continue watching the fire destroy all his possessions:

> As I watch, I realize that my whole life will change. I speak to the terrified man that I am in the dream, "There's no turning back now, No holding onto the past." But then I add a word of hope: "But keep waiting, your life isn't over."

> I'm not sure what I meant by this last word of encouragement, but it felt important, like "the past is gone, but the future is not destroyed."

Edward was surprised by his spontaneous words of advice to himself. He never expected to talk to himself in the revised dream, but he followed his impulse and crafted an unexpected revision.

Over the next few days, Edward kept rehearsing the ending, reminding himself, "the past is gone, but the future is not destroyed." He later told me, "It surprises me, but it's the first time I've felt any comfort about all that has happened."

After a couple of weeks, Edward began to feel that something more wanted to happen.

> I felt an impulse to go back into the revised dream and let it unfold more. This time I lingered and did what I've never been able to do in the nightmares: I see the dream all the way through and watch the fire burn away everything I possessed. Usually, I wake up while the house is still burning. But this time, I stayed in the scene. I didn't want to avoid it anymore, so I faced reality and let everything burn up as actually happened. Finally, there were only the last remaining hot embers.

Then I surprised myself. I have an impulse to call down "rain from heaven," like giving a blessing for all that I once had. "Now it's over," I said to myself, like giving a religious benediction. Then rain gently fell, and the smoke cleared. But I kept watching because it felt like something more wanted to happen. It's then that I saw a new house rise out of the ashes. It wasn't anything like the old one, which was very traditional. I was captivated because I sensed a mystical quality about this  new house like it's "a house from heaven." Those are the words that came to me, a sign of a new life waiting for me, one that I hadn't even realized was possible.

I'm left with a feeling of comfort and consolation for the first time since we lost our house several years ago.

Edward's creative response to his chronic nightmares exemplifies what can happen when someone allows their imagination to surprise them. His example, along with Robin's unexpected response to her tortuous critics, demonstrates the value of making a potent creative response. By way of review, the characteristics of an unexpected and effective response are as follows.

- Solve the problem. Don't create more.
- Let unexpected solutions come to you.
- Favor solutions that also work in waking life.
- Choose solutions that have the least amount of collateral damage.
- Stay genuine. Follow actions that are true to your deeper feelings.
- Experiment with a new role. Try stepping out of your usual way of behaving.

In the following chapters, you will see that I take traditional Image Rehearsal Therapy beyond its usual practice of simply re-writing nightmares to make them stop, and instead offer an enriched approach, one that explores the *meaning* of dreams. Here you seek to know the *purpose* of a nightmare. With this knowledge, you can then cooperate with Nature's intention when it orchestrates a particular dream for you.

———————————

Absorbing Difficult Truth

One of the most unwelcome aspects of dreams is that they often show us things we do not want to know. In this sense, the intelligence that orchestrates dreams might be likened to a tenacious friend. It means us no harm but is so committed to our welfare that it does not spare us painful realizations or indulge us in sentimental or false notions about ourselves or the world. In other words, there is something uncomfortably truthful about dreaming. It places a high value on reality; it prepares us to survive by helping us adapt to how things truly are.

The truth-bearing function of dreaming has been one of the most challenging aspects of dreamwork for me. Without a doubt, the realizations I have found through dreams have benefitted me and matured me into a wiser person. Still, these very insights also disrupted my ideal image of myself and challenged my illusory thinking.

An example of how dreams wrestle with us to bring us needed insights can be found in the film *Dreaming to Heal PTSD and Moral Injury* (www.evolutionarydreaming.com). It tells the story of a war veteran who repeatedly suffered nightmares of being chased by Iraqi citizens intent on harming him. The frequent intrusions at night resulted in sleep deprivation and debilitating headaches.

Before studying his dreams, the soldier assumed that his nightmares were simply a replay of the dangers he had lived with every day during the war. Like many suffering from chase dreams, he had never stopped to reflect on why those pursuing him were hostile and intent on harming him.

To deepen his understanding of the dream, I introduced the soldier to a method of dream investigation that would enable him to re-enter the memory of his dream in an awake state and pose questions and interact with dream figures. After coaching him on using his breath to calm and steady himself, I suggested that he return to the place in the dream where he would always wake up—just as he was about to be overtaken. "How about doing the unexpected?" I proposed. "Stop running, then turn and face the angry citizens chasing you and ask, "Why do you want to kill me?" I added, "Wait for your imagination to give you an idea of what they wish to say."

Desperate to get relief from his nightmares, the soldier followed my lead. He was shocked by the truth of what he heard. "I know why they want to kill me," he confessed. "It's for the harm I've done. I killed one of their own."

The soldier described how he had mistakenly shot a defenseless young Iraqi mother during a search for terrorists. He and his search team had suddenly burst into the woman's house. Finding her sitting alone before a TV, the soldier shouted for the woman to freeze. Shocked by the frightening intrusion of armed soldiers, she was paralyzed with fear. But after a moment, the woman sprang to her feet and rushed towards another room. On pure instinct, the soldier fired, dropping her to the floor. It was then that he realized why the woman had panicked and run. He heard the cry of the woman's baby coming from the other room.

Despite being told that he had done the right thing in the line of duty, the soldier carried guilt that he could not erase. It was his shame that he had to come to terms with, something that is a pervasive issue for many soldiers returning from war. The soldier suffered moral injury, a condition in which he had violated his conscience, his sense of right and wrong, and no amount of justification would relieve him. The soldier's conscience was pursuing him, symbolized by the avenging Iraqi citizens.

I have just introduced an important idea here that I want to make more apparent. The people (and animals and objects) in our dreams may represent hidden aspects of our personalities, though ones with which we are less familiar. This symbolic understanding of dream figures can explain why particular people, of all the thousands we have known, appear in our dreams. Each dream figure is composed of qualities that make them unique and distinctive, and they may show up in dreams to exemplify particular aspects of our personalities. In the case of the soldier, the avenging citizens represented the part of himself that was angry and self-punishing.

To find relief from his repetitive nightmares, the soldier had to find healing for his conscience. This required that he deepen his understanding of forgiveness, something he was not able to do alone. With my encouragement to share his painful truth with someone he trusted, he turned to his grandmother, a longtime compassionate advocate, and he found the great antidote to shame: empathy from someone who loved him. In this way, his nightmares ended.

This story illustrates how beneficial it can be to absorb a difficult truth. The soldier might have attempted to revise his dream with aggressive action, like killing those who pursued him. Fortunately, he had discovered the dream's purpose: to make him aware that he was running from his conscience. As a result, he found a far more effective solution than trying to escape. He discovered forgiveness for himself.

The Nightmare of Grief

In the following story, you see an example of a dream that only became a nightmare upon awakening. Carl, the dreamer, had separated from a woman with whom he had lived. He had attempted to put the memory of her out of his mind, and in his waking state, it appeared that he had succeeded. However, at night the woman came to him in his dreams. Upon awakening, the revived memory of the woman would set off profound feelings of grief and longing.

My first memory of Carl is that he was a surprisingly large man who blundered into my studio desperately seeking help for a reoccurring nightmare. He had called the afternoon before at the recommendation of a friend who said that I might help him with his disturbing dreams. The insistent tone in his voice, urging me to see him as soon as possible, conveyed that he was in trouble.

The force of Carl's knock on my door was jarring. I cautiously opened the door to a thick, tall man in his mid-fifties, who reached out with an oversized meaty hand and shook mine, clinching it with far more strength than necessary. At the same time, he stiff-armed me, pushing me back and away from him lest I overstep his wide boundaries. He rushed in with loud, heavy feet, moving aggressively towards a couch only a few feet away.

Foregoing typical protocols for getting acquainted, Carl started telling me about his distressing dreams before he had sat down. With unkempt hair, he looked as if he had just gotten out of bed. I imagined him to be at least 6'5", an imposing character whose belly overflowed his belt, which along with his commanding presence, made me immediately suspect that he was accustomed to having his way and getting more than his fair share of things.

Carl hastily sat down after setting a cup of coffee on the table in front of his seat. His knee jarred the table, and the coffee spilled. He did not stop talking as he wiped at the spill in one quick movement of his large hand, leaving a trail of

frothy milk behind. I imagined that everywhere he went, he must be leaving a trail of distress.

The most striking feature about Carl was his bluster. He spoke loudly, so much so that I instinctively pulled back from him in my chair. I had to address this right away since I feared that my office mates might be disturbed on the other sides of the walls. He lowered his voice but maintained his pressured, fast-paced speech.

"The problem is my dreams," Carl complained with an edge of irritation. "Damn it, I can't get her out of my mind. It happens a few times a month, and when it does, I'm fuckin' good for nothing all morning long." Carl had come to me to solve a problem, an inconvenience that disrupted his life. I detected no curiosity in him as to why he might be having the dreams, which he seemed to count more as a rude interruption to his busy life. He explained that when his former girlfriend appeared in his dreams, he couldn't return to sleep the rest of the night. Once in his office, an executive suite of glass walls that looked out onto his employees, he couldn't concentrate. "Eventually, I cancel my meetings for the next couple of hours and pull the blinds to get hold of myself. But shit..." Carl left it there as if he had given me my assignment. He added, "I'm pretty much useless 'till mid-day."

It had been a year since Carl had separated. His girlfriend of many years had "suddenly, out of the blue" told him that she couldn't "take it anymore." He portrayed her as having acted impulsively and without giving him fair warning, but when I imagined being his partner or business associate and having something to complain about, I felt dread. Carl was forceful, an alpha presence who had undoubtedly presumed that power and dominance would get him everything he wanted. Yet a chink in his armor had exposed a vulnerability, and he felt unnervingly defenseless as grief overtook him whenever he dreamed of his former love.

Carl kept a crowded schedule, traveled constantly, and had multiple superficial relationships with women since his girlfriend had left him. He seemed to have arranged his life so that the memory of her could not get to him. He never anticipated that she would follow him in his dreams.

I asked, "What happens in the dream?"

"Nothing," he said, seeming to stop short of a full explanation. I queried, "Nothing at all?"

"She just stands there looking at me," Carl insisted.

"What's the expression on her face?"

He looked away, studying the dream, silent for a moment. "She's just being herself, looking at me. No expression," he said matter-of-factly.

I knew that there was more to the picture than what Carl would or could describe. I remembered how it was the same for me when I was once overcome by protracted grief. I could not articulate any detailed description of my former love. I only felt the ache and longing.

I knew that I would have to help Carl identify the distinctive aspects of his girlfriend that made her poignantly disturbing to him. Like spreading out the pieces of a puzzle and noting what is unique about each one, I hoped to assist him in discerning the unique features that made his dream woman so compelling.

When we encounter a presence larger than us, one that captures our attention because it contains qualities needed in our development, we may very well be at a loss to describe what exactly it is that touches us. This is a common experience when someone is overcome by romantic love or grief. They are not able to name the particular qualities that make the other so commanding of their attention.

When I asked Carl to tell me about his former partner, he described her outer world; what she did rather than who she was: employment, education, and stories of their travels. She was "a great companion," he said. "I couldn't find anyone easier to travel with. Smart as hell, healthy, and responsible." There was nothing in Carl's description that helped either he or I make sense of the shock to his system whenever the woman appeared in his dreams.

Eventually, at a loss at discerning what this woman's personality was like, I asked Carl to show me photos of her. Opening his phone, he presented one taken when they were at sea on his yacht. Carl appeared to be the life of the party, beer in hand, laughing widely, lifting his Budweiser high in what might have been a victory salute to his rowdy friends. She, on the other hand, was off to the side, arms relaxed on the guard rail at the edge of the deck, standing alone in a bathing suit. Dark-skinned and much smaller than Carl's sprawling physique, she looked out to sea as calm as the distant horizon, appearing to be in a world of her own, more in nature than on the luxurious party boat.

In another picture, they were both dressed for a gala party. Carl wore a tux and at first glance his tall frame overpowered her, yet when I studied her, dressed in an elegant long gown, she held her place with the same distinctive expression on her face. The words "calm certainty" came to me.

Carl described her background. "She was born to immigrant parents from Mexico. Grew up poor," he added, his voice softening, which surprised me and gave me a glimpse of tenderness that lay under his brusque manner. "She came from humble roots, and she never forgot it. She's loyal," he continued. "Visits her parents every week, in spite of her place at the university."

Carl swiped through more pictures, then abruptly stopped, studying one in uncharacteristic silence. He moved from the edge of his seat where he had sat as if ready to pounce up at any moment and settled to the back of the couch for support. His face flushed; his eyes softened. "This one," he pointed. "This is the one that gets me. It's how she is in the dream."

Handing me his phone, I studied a close-up of her face. She again appeared unselfconsciously settled in herself. Unlike Carl, she was inwardly poised and did not appear to need confirmation from anyone. But there was another quality that I perceived. I have seen it a thousand times in the faces of people across the planet when they have lived close to poverty and adversity, tempered by the harsh demands and constraints of life. It was the lack of what was there that moved me: *the absence of entitlement.* Her face conveyed a different kind of power that Carl was unacquainted with because of his bluster.

"I see what you're missing about her, Carl." He looked at me surprised, expectantly. "It's her humility."

Still facing me, Carl's gaze left mine, turning inward. His body relaxed, taking in a large breath, then letting out a long sigh. I repeated, "It's her humility that I suspect you miss." A confirming silence met my words. Carl remained still. I eased back into my chair to give him room.

We must have sat quietly for one long minute as Carl privately jour-
neyed through his thoughts. I eventually got up and returned with a damp
towel and water. Wiping the table free of the traces of the spill, I replaced
his empty coffee cup with a glass of fresh water. He looked up at me as I
was still standing. "Is there room in your life for her, Carl?" His eyes questioned me. I posed a clarifying question, "How content and happy would
she be to follow you in your day, right there beside you, inside you?"

I reached over to where I had sat Carl's phone. I touched the screen,
and her picture returned. Turning it towards him, I posed the question
once more. "Is there room for her spirit to live inside you? Look at those
eyes. What do you see?"

"Someone who never has to prove herself."

"Yes, nothing to prove, nobody to be. Because she already is somebody."

I continued. "Rather than trying to forget her, best you pause several
times a day and remember this about her." I could tell the suggestion be-
fuddled Carl. I gave more guidance.

"I'm not talking about rekindling your love affair. I'm pointing to a trait
in her that appears to be important to you. Humility gives her the freedom to simply be as she is, not having to prove herself or be better than
she is, and as a consequence, you can see in her face the calm confidence
that radiates out of her eyes."

To ground the idea in a way that would be useful for Carl, I had him go
through the previous day from morning to evening. We reviewed conversations he had had. I asked, "Would she have been comfortable with how
you handled that person?" We talked about how he barked orders at his
staff and the irritability he showed a young cashier, still nervous and new
on her job. Posing an alternative, I asked, "How would your former love
have handled those situations?" Little more was needed to draw a contrast
between Carl's heavy-handed manner and the gentle, feminine presence
that treated others with respect.

Our discussion led Carl to see how extensive the changes were that
were being asked of him by his seemingly "pointless dreams." He sat back
on the couch again, solemn, contemplating the task presented to him. I
was relieved at his response. He could have resisted, breaking into sarcasm or distracting humor, or he might have quickly changed the topic.

Instead, Carl sat still, "accepting the verdict," a phrase that has come to mind more than once when I have observed someone enduring a dream's incisive assessment. I was hopeful for Carl. It appeared that he might have the capacity to trust and tolerate the sobering realizations necessary for him to benefit from his nightmares.

Carl left much quieter than when he had entered.

We met often over the following months, and I learned a great deal about why Carl had become boisterous and imposing. He had grown up under the shadow of a father for whom he could never be good enough. Carl over-compensated, becoming bold and brash, seeking to be the best while attempting to disprove a presumption that had formed in him early in life: that he was not enough.

Carl's nightmares of grief did not end immediately. They continued to haunt him for a good while. Now, however, he had a way to understand their purpose, so necessary if he were to cooperate with the dream's intention. From my perspective, Carl's troubling dreams were seeking to grow him into a new version of himself: self-accepting, less demanding of himself and others, and possessing a quiet self-containment. This transformation, however, would not be easy, for much was at stake. Attitudes that Carl had assumed to be necessary for his success in life now had to be questioned, perhaps relinquished. Arrogance, intimidation, and blustering confidence had to be set aside for a new presence that wanted to live in him. As I imagined the work ahead for Carl, I suspected that he would probably feel like a king being dethroned, having to forego his upper-handed positioning to make room for a softer side of himself, epitomized by the woman who looked at him in dreams with haunting, humble eyes.

Carl's story does not end here. We will pick it up again when we study the last step in the Nightmare Completion process discussed in the section Living the New Dream. As you will see, Carl began changing in ways he never thought possible, eventually developing the very qualities in himself that he so adored in the woman of his dreams. These changes did not come about easily because Carl first had to absorb difficult truths about attitudes and behaviors in himself that were contrary to the new man he was asked to be.

The Reason for Betrayal

I once knew a man who feared that his dreams were warning him of an imminent betrayal. Having never considered this possibility before, Daniel was shaken when his wife of fifteen years began to leave him for other men in his dreams. In the nightmares, he would be grief-stricken, and for

hours after, he could find no relief, making it impossible for him to concentrate on his work. He could not shake the possibility that his marriage was about to end. The dreams were so real that Daniel was sure that he was being warned of an impending affair. However, when he told his

wife of the betrayal dreams—even naming the various men —she denied any desire to leave Daniel and emphatically said one day, "I don't know what these dreams are about, but I can tell you that they aren't about me. I love you and have no interest whatsoever in complicating my life like that!" He wanted to believe her, and a part of him did, yet the nightmares continued.

Daniel was fiercely competitive in sports and business. From his perspective, the forcefulness of his willpower gave him his competitive edge and made it possible for him to retire at an early age and earn the respect and love of friends and family. From the dream's perspective, however, all was not well. The wife of his dreams was deeply discontented.

The answer to Daniel's nightmare dilemma came when he realized that the wife of his dream was symbolic of a side of himself that was displeased with the life he was leading. This part of him, his inner feminine nature, was no longer content to be ignored, and she had found a way (in the dreaming) to let her discontent be known.

As with Carl above, the solution for Daniel's nightmares was to develop qualities in himself that he had long neglected: vulnerability, tenderness, the expression of a wider range of feelings (not just anger and dominance), and other virtues that he valued in his wife. As often happens,

Daniels' transformation started with him first accepting sobering truths about himself.

Dreams About Things Long Ago

(Be advised that the following story contains references to sexual abuse, though the outcome is positive.)

When I was in my early fifties, I had a fleeting image in a dream of the black, 1953 Chevrolet that was our family's first car. Interestingly, the dream presented this car with my seeing it, not from the side or front, but the back.

Once awake and curious to know more, I remained still and lingered with the image. As I allowed my imagination free reign to take me where it wished, I found myself peering into the car through the back window, which then sparked a memory. I was suddenly transported back to early childhood, sometime between my fifth and eighth years. I remembered being in the back seat as my father, mother, and I rode home from church one night. I recalled how I burst out crying, no longer able to bear the tension of a secret that I had been holding.

A twelve-year-old neighborhood boy whom I trusted and looked up to had taken me on his paper route and allowed me to ride on the handlebars of his bicycle. I felt special. He stopped unannounced at a service station after delivering the newspapers and took me inside the bathroom with him. There he attempted sexual contact with me. As he undressed me and started to fondle me, I went into a protective freeze response, which caused the boy to realize that I would not be cooperative. He then abruptly stopped and took me home.

Three days later, on the way home from church in the backseat of that black 1953 Chevy, I broke into sobs under the weight of the shame and fright that I carried.

This was not a new memory. I had spoken of it several times with close friends and a therapist, but I had no idea that I was still under the lingering effects of this early trauma. As I recalled this pivotal event in my early life, I became aware that I carried tension throughout my body, but it was more than that. It felt like an electric charge was buzzing in me, and I instinctively knew it was related to the perpetration I had suffered and was now recalling because of the dream.

Knowing that the effects of trauma often remain with us until the body has been allowed to discharge them, I permitted my body to do whatever it needed. Breathing slower and fuller than usual, I relaxed and surrendered. As a result, I began to tremble and continued doing so for two or three minutes. Observing all this, I found myself surprised at how far-reaching the effects of my childhood abuse were. It was as if I had been carrying this negative impact my entire life but was only now aware of it.

After a few minutes, my body came to rest, and I felt at peace, though a feeling of melancholy remained. I took this mix of tenderness and sadness as a sign that I had finally—after some five decades—found my way to empathy for what I had suffered. I realized that while I had certainly felt embarrassed and sometimes ashamed when recounting my sexual abuse before—at times avoiding the subject altogether—I had never until this moment felt compassion for what my younger self had suffered.

I often remember this dream and the discharge that occurred when someone complains about dreams that bring back memories of being harmed. While my experience certainly does not compare in intensity to the overwhelming emotions stirred by those who suffered more extensive trauma, the process I am describing can still be instructive.

One way we cope with distressing events is by closing off awareness of what we are feeling. This is a dissociative process, much like numbing ourselves so that we are not overwhelmed by a flood of physical and emotional pain. We can see this most pointedly when someone has been seriously injured, maybe suffering a broken bone, but is in the early stages of shock and does not feel pain.

While there are untold benefits from this protective mechanism, there are lingering side effects that may leave us, even unbeknownst to ourselves, impaired in subtle or drastic ways. For example, with sexual abuse, there may be a dampening of sensual experience or a restricting of sexual feelings to physical stimulation while disengaged from tenderness and love.

As mentioned in the earlier chapter, *The Crucial Step*, Nature appears to be alarmed—if I for a moment can ascribe to Nature what it feels—about us closing off any capacity to feel. It seems to want us to be uncompromised by distressing past events so that we can be fully present in the moment and thus accurately respond to and participate in life as it is now. For this reason, dreams bring our awareness to past adverse events when we have closed off our feelings or conversely have become so hyper-activated around an issue that we no longer respond accurately to life as it is today.

It helped that I knew to trust and follow the discharge that my body wanted when I recalled my traumatic experience. It was also helpful to remember that recalling a difficult truth from my childhood was intended to help me. By finally and fully processing the harm done to me, I was able to absorb the trauma and neutralize its lingering effects.[4].

The Art of Soberness

The above stories illustrate the benefits of absorbing difficult truths. The sobering knowledge that dreams press on us can free us from the lingering effects of past hurt or help us change attitudes and behaviors that limit us from experiencing a fuller life. However, as mentioned previously, this truth-telling function of dreams has been by far the most unpleasant and, at times, unnerving aspect of dreamwork for me.

There have been many mornings after awakening that I have dreaded opening my laptop (or dream journal) to record the details of a dream. Such difficulty is often because the acceptance of a dream's sobering truth frequently requires that we allow for emotions we have avoided, as illustrated by my dream above which recalled past trauma. Or the knowledge imposed on us by a dream may lead to a downsizing of our idealized

---

4. One of the more useful authors I have read about allowing the body to complete trauma is Peter Levine (2008), who has written extensively and provides wonderful training in a therapeutic process called Somatic Experiencing.

self-image. We discover humbling things about ourselves. This is particularly difficult to tolerate if you are inclined to perfectionism and thus feel undue shame when mistakes are exposed. Such an encounter can be demoralizing.

Of course, there is a solution for this: being generous-hearted with yourself. In fact, I would say that if you are frugal with the amount of forgiveness that you extend to yourself, it will be exceedingly difficult, if not torturous at times, to do dreamwork. On the other hand, if you can bring someone to mind who is gracious towards you, as the grandmother was for the soldier above who suffered injury to his conscience, then it is much easier to absorb the difficult truths that dreams bring.

Dreams are often difficult because they bring us face to face with shame, either the shame that comes when we have been violated, an experience that is common when victimized, or the inevitable shame that comes when we realize we have harmed another. While it is popular today to view all shame as bad, I feel that there is an evolutionary advantage to this most difficult of emotions, particularly when we have hurt someone else. Shame sobers us, and if allowed, it can induce empathy in us for how we have harmed another. It can cleanse us of self-centeredness. However, shame can just as often be toxic and can undermine our basic dignity. Thus, there is an art to bearing the sobering truth of dreams, especially when shame is involved.

In my view, we do best if we work with shame similar to how we ride a bicycle; staying in the middle, not going too far to one side or the other. If we are naive to shame, we can easily succumb to debilitating self-reproachment, but if we are trite and dismissive, we forgo shame's potential to mature us. Admittedly, the dance between extremes can be challenging, But therein lies the art of soberness.

The most graceful human beings I know are those who can truthfully embrace the difficulties of life and of themselves without denial while also holding empathy for the complexity in which we all inevitably find ourselves. The story below illustrates the strength, humility, and delicate balancing that is required when we venture into a depth of self-examination that has the potential to add immense value to our lives but which can also, in a moment, entrap us in paralyzing regret and shame.

A Ritual of Bowls

Arlene had just sat down with her eldest daughter to enjoy a Mother's Day lunch at her favorite restaurant. Although she lived in the same city as both of her daughters, she had not seen her firstborn for over a year. Arlene thus anticipated that her daughter's gesture of asking her to lunch, something never before offered, was a hopeful sign that her daughter's longstanding coldness towards her might be waning. Instead, the twenty-eight-year-old who was already seated and waiting startled her mother as soon as she sat down. Without exchanging a greeting or embrace, the daughter abruptly announced, "I've got a few things to get off my chest today."

It was "a disastrous conversion," Arlene recalled. "The hostility was so intense that I could barely take in what she said." In the daughter's eyes, her mother had "miserably failed."

This was not the first time that Arlene's daughter had complained. There had been numerous prior episodes of her suddenly storming out of the house and shouting insults behind her as she slammed the door. This time, however, she sat upright across from her mother and listed one incident after another, "a torrent of crimes," Arlene later recounted, in which the embittered daughter had felt betrayed and neglected as a child.

Arlene was barely able to breathe. Her chest constricted in fear. With her face turned down, shame began to immobilize her. "There was truth in everything she said," Arlene admitted, "and I knew I needed to digest it, but how do you do that when you fear drowning in waves of unworthiness and regret? I despised myself and was filled with self-loathing. I wanted to disappear, but I knew I must respond. At that moment, the only thing I knew to do was to agree with her. 'Yes, that's true,' I said. But then, in an attempt to save myself from losing all dignity, I added, 'But I can't change the past.' This only enraged her all the more."

In the weeks that followed, Arlene was plunged into depressive self-reproachment, a downward pull that she could not lift out of, nor did she want to, she said. "I knew that I had to get to the heart of how I had injured my daughter, not just to feel bad about it, but to understand how it happened. To do this, I realized that I had to be compassionate towards myself; otherwise, I would never see all the conditions that had led to me having neglected her."

Knowing how tedious such a process of self-examination could be, Arlene settled on a ritual that would keep her balanced and protect her from getting lost in self-dejection.

"I was in the jungle of Ecuador at the time, having just flown there to a healing retreat center shortly after the Mother's Day disaster. I knew that I had a huge task before me, but I felt stymied about how I would ever navigate the treacherous emotional terrain that lay before me. Following a teacher's suggestion, I found two clay pots and gathered many small stones, and finally, when ready, I sat underneath a large tree beside a gentle-flowing stream for several hours each day. In one pot, I would throw a stone and let myself remember something my daughter had accused me of. Rather than run from the painful realization of how I had neglected her or had been preoccupied with my turbulent life, I took in my daughter's perspective so that I could understand why she felt such anger towards me. When I had absorbed as much as I could, I then turned to the other pot and threw in a stone to remind me of something good in our relationship, a special moment we had enjoyed, something that kept me remembering the goodness that had also been in my mothering of her."

For several days, Arlene continued the ritual, keeping each bowl evenly filled as she went back and forth between the painful realizations of how she had unknowingly let her daughter down to then remembering the love and goodness that had also existed. "Eventually, I began to see things from my own childhood that had contributed to my later difficulty in parenting. I realized how the effects of my own early abuse—beatings from my father, a rape by an older acquaintance which I couldn't describe to anyone, and emotional coldness from my mother—had left me in a depressed state as a young mother. Gradually, a feeling of compassion for the whole situation of my life began to settle over me. I knew then that I must learn to stay attentive to my daughter whenever she would rage at me so that I could acknowledge her pain. But at the same time, I realized that I had to be very careful not to give way to debilitating self-judgment, which would only lead me into depression."

As a result of Arlene's life review, which required both courage and skill, she found fortitude in the months that followed when conflict erupted between her and her daughter. "I can stay present now," she confided to me.

"How?" I asked.

"I maintain eye contact and don't flinch away from her criticism. I acknowledge her perspective. At the same time, I don't succumb to shame. That's always overwhelmed me before and robbed me of being able to hear my daughter out."

"And the effects of this?" I asked.

"We repair quicker. She comes back to me sooner when there's conflict between us. But just as importantly, I don't forsake my dignity when bearing the truth of mistakes I've made."

Arlene's ritual of the bowls, and her earnestness to be thorough and truthful, inspires me. However, I am just as moved by her savviness in navigating what she described as a "treacherous emotional terrain," a place where she could have easily lost her footing and remained in despair.

In telling Arlene's story, I am reminded of the invaluable advice a dear friend gave me when I was teetering above a chasm of self-recrimination. "Don't give up your birthright," he cautioned me, referring to the inalienable right to be forgiven. "Otherwise, how will you learn if you don't make mistakes, even seemingly tragic mistakes? And how would any of us ever know the depths of unconditional love if we did not ever so often lose our way?"

Knowing Your Adversary

Not all dream figures that frighten us intend to harm us. In my opinion, this is the most misunderstood dynamic of dreaming. Threatening dream figures are often representations of hidden potentials of our personalities that have not been allowed to develop and be expressed. They may contain attributes and qualities that were off-limits to us earlier in life. Consequently, when we encounter these very forces in our dreams, we feel threatened.

As mentioned in the first chapter, I came to realize the importance of discerning whether a threatening dream figure was attempting to help me or hurt me when I dreamed of bushmen from Africa breaking into my house. I will now go into more detail to describe the tools I used to investigate this dream. The understanding I found proved to be pivotal in helping me mature my masculinity. As a reminder, I will summarize the dream below.

> I dream that I'm safely resting in my bed when I hear someone opening the window to my bedroom. Alarmed, I look over to my right, and I'm shocked to see an African bushman, a warrior, climbing through my bedroom window with a spear in hand, dressed only in a loincloth. I happen to have a gun in bed with me, one given to me in childhood, and I use it to kill the intruder, but I am dismayed because after the man collapses, another climbs in. After killing the second intruder, a third follows, whom I also kill, but then a fourth enters. I wake up in a panic when I realize that in spite of killing one after the other, there will be no end to these determined invaders. Overcome by terror, I awake in a panic.

Once I overcame my shock, I was bewildered. "Why would I dream of men from a culture far removed from the life I know? And even more disconcerting, why would they be breaking into my bedroom?" Fortunately, the dream came when I first

started studying with my therapist, so I had her help in discovering what these men symbolized. She posed a question that I have used countless times since whenever I wish to explore the meaning of a dream figure: "What makes these men unique and distinctive?" she asked.

Two characteristics stood out to me.

- They lived close to nature and followed their instincts in order to survive.
- They carried a spear with them and thus had a means of defending themselves.

Of course, I might have named other qualities, but these are the ones that impressed me the most. Based on this, I then described my intruders as *primal warriors*.

Having named the defining qualities of my dream figures, I then compared myself to them. Unlike these robust men, I realized that I often lived in my head, pondering decisions much longer than necessary. I didn't trust or follow my instincts.

Secondly, I did not carry a spear; that is, I did not have the means of safeguarding myself. I was not direct. When bothered, I withdrew. As I further compared myself to these warriors, I had to admit to another negative characteristic: I carried an air of aloofness. By contrast, I imagined that my warriors did not need to be cautious and reserved the way that I was because they had the means of protecting themselves. Because I had no spear, that is, because I had not learned to speak up with the directness and pointedness of a spear, I protected myself by maintaining distance.

My god-fearing parents sought to instill a strict moral code in me; to obey authority and be compliant. I was unfamiliar with navigating conflict. While I had certainly been exposed to conflict growing up, I did not have one memory of seeing my parents resolve an argument through conversation. In fact, my father became known for a classic line when a disturbance would break out between him and my mother. As soon as he would hear my mother's complaining voice, he would get up and leave the room, uttering his standby defense just before he slammed the door behind him: "Just forget about it, Evelyn." With that, he would turn the TV on in another room or make his way to the isolation of his garden. I never saw my father stand up, speak for himself, and resolve conflict through discussion.

At the time of the dream, I did not know I was compromised and without a sure means of protecting and advocating for myself. The dream of the primal warriors might have been my first clue. In fact, it took me some painful years to make sense of my quick and unexpected withdrawal of affection after I would draw close to a woman and begin to develop ties of intimacy. Strangely, my romantic feelings would disappear in a short while. At the time, I had no clue that it had to do with my ill-preparedness to speak up on my behalf, to advocate for what I needed, and to address issues that bothered me. I protected my autonomy and my self-hood, by becoming emotionally distant. Of course, this led to a safe but lonely life.

As I look back now, the dream of the warriors was one of the first signs of my instincts breaking through to rescue me from my life-limiting patterns of passivity. The bushmen presented me with a view of primal masculinity, something I sorely needed but which also intimated me. At the time, I had no idea that I lacked anything, and the absence of this awareness led to some painful breakups with good and remarkable women and the loss of friends. But eventually, I caught on. I started observing some of my friends who knew how to speak up and articulate their feelings. They stood square to the ground, held their own, and did not resort to explosive attacks on another nor retreat from the heat of disagreement. I learned by carefully watching how they handled conflict, and I owe a great deal to them for my self-development, including the ability to sustain love.

For these reasons, the nightmare of the intruding bushmen remains one of the most helpful dreams that I have had, for it showed me an unrealized potential that I did not even know that I needed. While initially appearing to be my enemies, the intruding warriors eventually proved to be some of my best mentors.

Getting to the Essence of a Dream Figure

The above dream illustrates how beneficial it can be to identify the essential qualities of a dream figure. (Of course, what you find to be noteworthy may differ from what someone else would identify.) By naming the characteristics of dream figures, you de-literalize them, decipher their symbolic meaning, and thus make them beneficial to you. Without this, you are left with vague notions of a dream figure's relevance. Or, like many, you may be tempted to revert to a dictionary of dream symbols and read conflicting opinions of what a symbol means, ideas which more than likely do not have enough specificity for you and your individual life. The method of identifying the unique, distinguishing qualities of a dream figure, as I did with the bushmen, is an invaluable way to get to the heart of a dream figure's importance for you. I refer to this investigative method as *Distilling the Essence*.

There is another way of acquiring more information about a dream figure than what was initially in the dream. It is an investigative method known as *Let Dream Presences Speak*. Once you are awake, it is possible to re-enter the memory of the dream and pose questions to dream figures to learn what they are like and why they have appeared to you. Let me give an example of this. It is the dream of Emily, a woman in her early forties who dreamed of a scene that reminded her (upon awakening) of a traumatic event she had undergone several years earlier.

The dream:

> I am lost in a heavily wooded forest, and I'm terrified. A man is stalking me, and I fear for my life.

Though the dream was brief, the impact was startling. Emily's hands trembled when she told me the scant details a few hours later. Memories of her past flooded her, insisting, it seemed to me, that she no longer avoid a truthful recounting of how badly she had suffered. One memory was particularly poignant. Her former abusive husband had chased her

 down when she once attempted to escape in her car. He drove her off the road and then brought her back to their house, where he waited for nightfall. When darkness descended, giving the man the secrecy he wanted, he led Emily into the

woods behind their home and bound her hands and feet with rope, leaving her alone and terrified in the night. The traumatic impact of this incident had left Emily afraid of ever being in the woods after that.

Upon hearing the story, my heart sank at the details of the cruel treatment. As any good therapist or friend knows, when hearing such an account of harm, you give all the time necessary for tender, vulnerable feelings to be acknowledged and consoled. And so I did. Yet, I wondered to myself, "Is this what the dream had in mind, to revive Emily's painful memories? Or did the dream have another purpose when it orchestrated this riveting drama?" I did not know, but I knew that we could go back to the dream and study it for more details.

Once Emily's emotions had settled, I asked if we could get a closer look at who was in the dream with her. She had assumed a male had followed her, intending to do her harm, but beyond that, she had no more details. I suggested that Emily go back into the dream, now that she was awake and safe with me, and let her imagination show her more. She quieted herself, closed her eyes, returned to the memory of the dream, and posed a decisive question, "Who *are* you?"

Emily was immediately surprised. "No," she reported to me. "It wasn't my ex at all. Yes, he's strong and potentially ferocious, but this man means me no harm."

"How do you know this?" I asked, as surprised as she was.

Emily closed her eyes again and allowed her spontaneous imagination to give her more information. "He's rugged and can be fierce if needed," she explained, " like someone who has lived in the jungle his whole life." She then became tearful and spoke tenderly, making an admission that again surprised both of us. "He's come to protect me."

After having just learned of Emily's tortuous experience in her former marriage, I, too, became tearful at the unexpected kindness pursuing her. "So," I offered, "you have

glimpsed a side of yourself, your protective warrior. He's a picture of a hidden potential in you that's finally awakened and is ready to serve you."

Shortly after the dream, Emily found a man who trained her in self-defense. He was barely five feet tall, and like Emily, had been bullied as a child. Once older, however, he sculpted his muscles and skills into that of a formidable mixed-martial artist. Perhaps because of his diminutive stature, he exuded a message poignantly relevant for his trainee: "*Just because you were made to feel small, you need not live the rest of your life that way.*"

As Emily practiced self-defense, she became acquainted with the power in her body, leading her to an unexpected fascination with gorillas: their strength, their size, and most of all, their roar. Once Emily demonstrated to me what *her* gorilla sounded like. "Do you want to hear?" she playfully asked. Not knowing what would befall me, I naively answered, "Yes, of course." The normally meek and gentle woman stood up with her feet apart and planted firmly on the ground. She inhaled deeply and then let out a warning cry that could be heard down the corridors of the office where we were. Her wild animal roar caused the hairs on the back of my neck to stand up.

A Word of Caution

In mentoring dreamers over the years, including psychotherapists, I have observed that a common mistake people make is quickly relating the details of the dream to something in waking life. This happened initially with Emily, who immediately assumed that her dream of being in a forest pertained to past trauma. It is tempting to assume that disturbing dreams are symbolic replications of traumatic events when someone has been traumatized. Therapists are especially in danger of presuming this when working with clients diagnosed with PTSD. Of course, this is understandable if someone like Emily has a strong emotional response to a dream that evokes painful memories.

Of course, we must respectfully attend to any recall of traumatic events triggered by a dream. However, we should be careful not to assume that the dream intends to revive a traumatic memory just because someone recalls an adverse event upon awakening. While waking life associations to the dream may prove helpful, they are not necessarily what a dream intends to do with a dreamer.

By staying close to the details of the dream, as I did when I asked Emily to go back and verify who the man was in the woods with her, we may discover invaluable information that indeed surprises us.

The dream of the protective warrior is one of many dreams I have heard that first appear to be referencing past trauma. However, when attended to more closely, it becomes evident that the intimidating dream figure is bringing the dreamer into contact with potentials that can ultimately help them deal with and overcome trauma. You will see another example of this in the following two dreams: a bear pursued me and would not leave me alone.

A Bear Stalks Me

Some years ago I was terrified by the appearance of a bear in my dreams. Here's how I described the first dream in my journal.

I am walking up a steep path on the side of a mountain when I see a bear several hundred feet above me coming towards me. Alarmed, I turn back and retreat, eventually finding refuge in a house where three women live whose identity I do not know. But despite hiding inside, my fear doesn't subside. I remain terrified that the bear will eventually find me. Unable to stand the dread any longer, I wake up in a panic.

The encounter with the bear disoriented me. "Why was I so intimidated by this animal after having followed my dreams for several years?" I mused disquietly. I felt ashamed of myself for having acted so cowardly in the dream. Therefore, after my morning tea, I regained my confidence and began journaling my thoughts, determined to uncover what was at the heart of my fearful encounter.

I presumed that the bear was symbolic of a potential that I was not living. "Perhaps I'm lacking the boldness of a bear," I considered. This idea caused me to realize that indeed I had not given public talks in a long while, "perhaps," I imagined, "from having fallen back into a reclusive, shy side of my personality." I immediately pulled out my calendar and scheduled a series of presentations.

Thinking that I had found the meaning of my dream and heeded its message, I was dismayed a few weeks later when I had an even more terrifying encounter with the bear.

I'm walking through my house. Upon opening the door to my bedroom, I'm startled. A giant bear is sitting in the middle of my bed waiting for me, only this time its body is twice the size of even the largest of bears. Its mas-  sive furry body presses up against all four walls, and from this, I know that its head must be pressing against the ceiling as well. I wake up in horror.

I awoke from the dream with a perplexing question: "How could I have had another frightening bear dream?" I felt defeated. I had to admit that I had not done the work of the earlier dream. Otherwise, the bear would not have come a second time, and not only that, it would not have had to present itself so terrifyingly larger than before.

The dismay I felt shows how unrealistic we can be in our evaluation of ourselves. I presumed that I was much further along in my development than what the dream showed. I thought of myself as a courageous man. Given where I had started in life, I had excelled beyond my expectations. Unlike my relatives, I had graduated from college and established a professional career. I was athletic and had stayed fit and physically strong. I even recalled that I had parachuted twice on my fortieth birthday, and though terrified at the time, I persisted and did not retreat in fear. Yet, judging by my behavior in the dream, I had to admit that I acted like a frightened man.

The disparity between how we think of ourselves and how the dream assesses us can be great. As a result, our idealized self-image can be severely challenged by a dream. For this reason, we may feel ambivalent about studying dreams and complain, "Why pay attention to something that will humble and sober me?" We may be tempted to comfort ourselves by dismissively concluding, "Oh, it was only a dream."

By the time of my encounters with the bear, I knew that I should not ignore a humbling dream. There was something essential for me to know. So, I returned to the basics of dreamwork: I considered that the bear might be a picture of an unlived potential. I thus sought to distill its essence to see what qualities I might actualize. To do this, I re-entered the memory of the dream, switched roles, and imagined myself as the bear. I immediately felt its massive strength and confidence. I was surprised to feel how it lacked intimidation. By contrast, I realized that I did not feel this way much of the time. Despite my accomplishments, I still harbored underlying anxiety. The bear lacked this uncertainty. I realized that if I felt this way, I would presume to have a right to "take my place in the world," just as the bear does in its habitat.

Now with a more honest appraisal of myself, I admitted to a feeling I had carried for many years: I had not lived up to my potential. I often felt that I was on the sidelines of life, watching, not fully participating, cautiously holding back from full involvement. "Why would this be?" I asked.

A memory surfaced from when I was eight years old. My father had ragefully beaten me. The bruises on my legs had lasted for more than a week. He had been told that I had thrown a rock and bloodied the head of a neighbor girl, and as a result, he found me hiding under my bed, pulled me out, and punished me.

I had indeed thrown the rock, but I had never intended to hurt the girl who was my friend. We were on opposite sides in a game of war along with other neighborhood kids. The rock I had thrown was my imaginary hand grenade which I tossed towards the enemy, never thinking I would do harm. But when I saw blood running down the face of my friend, I was shocked and ran home, already knowing that I would be in trouble. I hid under my bed, where my father eventually found me. He yanked me out by one leg and turned me over on his lap. Pulling my trousers down to expose my bare legs, he beat me with his belt, never once inquiring of me as to what had happened.

While I had never lost this memory, I had not realized the full implications of my traumatic experience. However, this became apparent as I allowed my imagination to show me more about the bear dreams. Another memory surfaced. I was fourteen years old, and it was the end of the school year. My baseball team was playing against our rival. The game was near the end, the last half of the last inning. We were at-bat, and to our advantage, we had three players on base, but we were also behind 4-1. Two batters had already struck out, meaning that the next batter could either strike out and lose the game or conceivably hit a home run and win the game.

The coach waved the next batter away as he came towards home plate, knowing he was a weak hitter and would likely strike out. Coach Brown looked over at the rest of us sitting on the bench, considering who had the best chance of getting on base and driving in more runs. I saw his eyes land on me, his first choice, but before he could wave his hand for me to come forward, I turned my face away for fear that if I were chosen, I would surely lose the game. *I never tried for fear of making a mistake.*

In recalling this memory, I could see that the severe beating I had suffered stole my bear-like nature. The merciless punishment had sent a chill through my personality and had caused me to draw back from life and develop a cautiousness so that I would never make such a tragic error again.

These memories and insights, while sobering, gave me compassion for myself and helped me to be more understanding of my shyness whenever it was time in adult life to come to the plate and take a swing. Of course, I would be wary of making mistakes, given the injustice I had suffered as a boy.

The bear dreams, though initially upsetting, made me hopeful. Unlike my first impressions when I encountered the bear in my dreams, I understood that it had come to save me from a partially lived life. By bringing me face to face with my unrealized potential, pictured as the large and capable bear, I was given an image of the confidence that was possible for me to live.

Over the years, I have recalled the bear countless times, especially when tempted to draw back from life out of shyness or a feeling of inferiority. Remembering it has bolstered my courage as I realize that I am more than my trauma. The bear now reminds me of my resilience, the undamaged part of me capable of moving beyond my earlier ordeals.

When Dream Figures Are Actually Against You

Thus far, I have illustrated how frightening dream figures are often misunderstood to be adversaries intent on harming us, when, in fact, they are sometimes our advocates who have come to help us. In the next chapter, we will turn our attention to dream figures that are symbolic of forces in the personality that do wish to harm us. Such dreams may bring us face to face with people who have hurt us in the past, or they may confront us with hostile strangers who symbolize self-critical attitudes that undermine us. Like a medical x-ray, these dreams expose life-limiting attitudes or beliefs in need of being recognized and thus neutralized.

Recognizing Undermining Influences

An unexpected benefit of studying dreams is that they reveal hidden attitudes and patterns of behavior that are working against you. Dreams have the uncanny ability to pinpoint negative influences in your personality that limit you from being a better, more robust version of yourself. However, there is a price to pay for such wisdom. You have to sacrifice your pride and endure humbling realizations.

I was shocked when I first realized the sobering function of dreams. When I began studying my dreams with the help of my therapist, I expected that I would learn to unravel the fascinating and mysterious puzzles that dreams were. I thought that I would approach dreams much like a Sherlock Holmes investigator, cleverly observing obscure details to connect the dots and thus solve the mystery of why I had dreamed something so odd and perplexing. Instead, more times than not, I was confronted with truths that humbled me to the core.

An example of this comes from a dream I had in which I was trying to escape a prison compound guarded by Nazi soldiers. The dream terrified me because I saw no way out of my captivity.

I'm inside a barbed wire fence surrounding a camp of prisoners, reminding me of a WWII Nazi work camp. It is night, and I have furtively stolen my way to the outside of a building where I hide while peering around one corner closest to the gate where I hope to escape. A guard stands high above me, commanding a searchlight from a watchtower. Another soldier stands nearby at ground level with a rifle in his hands. I see that he is cold and heartless, ready to kill anyone who dares to break free.

At the time of the dream, I was experienced enough to know that dreams, like x-rays, give us knowledge of what lies within. Therefore, I awoke with a sickening feeling when I imagined that the dream reflected an imprisonment of which I was unaware. Aghast, I protested, "How could such oppressive forces live in me?" Contrary to what the dream portrayed, I saw myself as a gentle man, the opposite of a heartless prison guard.

I initially felt intimidated to study the dream, so I took time to quiet myself, imagining that I was breathing love in and out of my heart—a formidable practice for establishing a feeling of safety. Once I felt secure, I turned my attention to the soldier standing closest to me. I needed to understand him. Having generated a feeling of compassion for myself, I turned my empathy towards him to understand what had led him to become the cold, heartless man he was. (This is an example of how to investigate dream figures and collect more information about them than what was presented in the original dream.)

I studied the soldier, and I perceived no human warmth in him. It appeared that his sole capacity and mission in life was to punish and imprison.

Seeking deeper understanding, I wondered, "What led this man to become so heartless?" Again, utilizing the power of empathy as an investigative instrument, I posed the question directly to him, "What happened to you? You were once a young, soft, and tender boy. How did you become hardened?"

Following the investigative method of Let Dream Presences Speak[5], I waited for impressions to form in me. My imagination then provided these details: the soldier had been cruelly mistreated by his ruthless father. Such harsh treatment had closed the soldier's heart. What choice did he have? He survived daily humiliation by numbing himself to pain. Now I understood the soldier's coldness—it was his protective insulation to endure the daily insults he had suffered in childhood.

Next, I turned my attention from the soldier towards myself, searching to see where such heartlessness might live within me: "In what ways am I like him?" (Honest self-examination like this is best done by first connecting to a feeling of empathy for yourself.)

---

5. Let Dream Presences Speak is one of several investigative tools I describe in my book, Your Dream's Ten Best Friends (2022).

In response to my question, memories immediately came to mind in which I had acted harshly with children. I recalled how sternly I had reproached a good friend's young daughter who had refused to eat anything on her plate. Another memory reminded me how the intimidating tone of my voice had frightened the young son of one of my relatives. I recalled the fearful freeze that came over the child's face when I commanded him to do something, which now I can't even recall. It certainly was not a life-threatening issue. But at the time, I felt justified in acting with heavy-handed authority, and in fact, I remembered that I even felt it was my duty to "subdue" the young child's willfulness.

Other memories followed. No physical punishment was involved, yet none was required to intimidate and "put the child back in their place," which was how I thought of and justified my behavior at the time. I found it challenging to stay with the sobering scenes, for they caused me sorrow and shame. Yet, I knew that I must tolerate the humbling realizations of what I had done to innocence. Had I not first grounded myself in a feeling of love, I could not have stayed with this forthright examination.

The empathy I had used to know the backstory of the heartless guard proved helpful, for it enabled me to turn the same compassionate inquisitiveness towards myself. I thus posed the same question to me that I had asked of the soldier: "What happened to you? You were once a young, soft, and tender boy. How did you become the man who has acted so ruthlessly?"

In response to my inquiry, the memory of my father's abuse of me came to mind—an experience I described in the previous chapter *Knowing Your Adversary*. I was just eight years old when my father found me hiding under my bed after I had thrown a rock towards a group of neighborhood kids in a game of war. He beat me mercilessly without ever inquiring as to why I had thrown a rock that struck the head of one of my friends. Now tracing the relevance of the Nazi guard dream, I recalled the terror that overwhelmed me when I heard the rageful, guttural sounds, not even words, coming out of my father's throat as he pulled me from my hiding place and lashed me with his belt. I remembered how I had gone numb that day, just like the Nazi guard had when he endured humiliations from his father.

Other memories came, including violence by my mother's father. I was even younger, perhaps five years old, when in a rage, my grandfather ripped the cord off of a nearby iron and used it to whip me. He prevented my escape by seizing me with his strong farmer's hand, and holding my arm above my head, he whipped my body. The pain and shock were so great and unexpected that I disassociated, leaving my body and witnessing the frightening spectacle from above.

Over the years, I have tried to make sense of my grandfather's harsh treatment, wondering what had incited him to such violence. The only clue is a memory of me impudently spitting on my grandfather just before he whipped me, certainly a show of pure, child-like protest for which I had no words.

I then remembered more. Around the time of the beating, I was playing on the floor, sitting in the middle of a doorway be-tween two rooms of my grandparent's farmhouse. My grandfather walked past me, going from one room to another, and without warning, he in-tentionally stepped on my hand, letting the full weight of his heavy boot down on my innocent fingers spread open to the floor. "Let that be a les-son to you," he said, reprimanding me sternly as I looked up at him with a tearful and shocked face. "Whenever an adult walks through the room, you get out of their way."

I no longer remember the chronology of events—whether this hap-pened before or after the beating—but the memory verified how harsh and punitive the atmosphere was that my defenseless child-self lived in when visiting my grandparents.

As I recalled these events, sorrow swept over me for how I had been mistreated and had subsequently perpetuated harshness onto others as innocent as I had been. I understood how I had become like the heartless prison guard. I was humbled.

I allowed these sobering realizations to melt the numbness around my heart that had initially protected me from the pain of my father's and grandfather's abuse. I realized that the protective numbing had cut me off from tender feelings for myself, dulling my empathic connection to myself and eventually others, thus making me capable of inflicting harm.

After allowing the flood of memories, along with their sobering realizations, I returned to the dream and remembered another disturbing fact: I was an imprisoned man. The dream had cast me in an insufferable role, showing that I was under an authority not my own. With trepidation, I asked, "What could this mean?"

Using the dream as a metaphor, a picture of my inner situation, I recognized how the harsh, punitive forces that had been turned on me as a child continued to live in me as severe self-criticism. The harshness of my father and grandfather had imprinted itself in me, as traumatic experiences do. Now I understood why I often could not enjoy the satisfaction of work well done. A critical eye would intrude and cause me to feel that nothing I did was good enough.

The sobering life review initiated by the prison dream was, of course, challenging to do, but it proved to be helpful in an unexpected way. In the weeks and months that followed, I became more adept at recognizing when the critical eye was turned on me.

The dream of my imprisonment demonstrates how disturbing dreams can be beneficial. It gave me a riveting *experience* of being held hostage, an event that made an impression on me far more than even the most trusted of friends encouraging me to be easier on myself. As a result, the frightening encounter has helped me intervene in an underlying pattern of harsh criticism, both towards myself and others. Though humbling, the dream proved deeply restorative. With uncanny precision, it helped me realize unseen forces in my personality that were undermining me. And for this reason, I am grateful for its sobering truth.

When an Abuser Reappears

One of the more disturbing aspects of nightmares is when an abuser from the past appears in a dream. To appreciate why this occurs and how you can cooperate with the dream's intention, it will help to understand a psychological dynamic called introjection.

It is commonly known that children absorb the qualities of those important to them, particularly parents and caregivers. In this way, they incorporate the values and characteristics of influential people into their lives. The internalization of the qualities of people in a child's life is a natural form of rapid learning and is essential for a child to mature. However, what is less known is that people who exert a harmful effect on us can also be incorporated (introjected) into the personality, even as adults. This is especially true when the harm inflicted on us is painful and intense, as happens in traumatic events.

Dreams bring us face to face with hostile forces we have unknowingly internalized. As medical imaging reveals underlying disease processes, so dreams can reveal negative imprints that are active in the personality. You can see an example of this in the above dream of the Nazi guards who were symbolic of harsh forces I had internalized.

After having just read of the abuse I suffered from my grandfather, you will now be able to appreciate the alarm I felt when I dreamed of him some forty years after he harmed me. (Note: The following account describes racist violence.)

The dream opens with me walking across a field. I feel apprehension, sensing that someone is following me.

I stop and turn to see who or what is pursuing me. It is my grandfather, a man whom I had feared throughout my childhood due to his critical nature and his harsh, abusive treatment of me as a young boy. I am surprised to see him, but

even more, I am shocked when I look into his face: it is as monstrous and grotesque as any horror figure I have ever seen.

The dream troubled me for many weeks and caused me to realize just how much I still feared my grandfather. At the time, I was well beyond childhood, and I had seemingly put the past behind me. I had become polite and respectful of my grandfather at family gatherings, though I kept my distance. However, the dream showed me that the effect of his harsh treatment still lingered in me, and I needed to face it. I feared him so much that he was like a monster to me.

I had little idea what to do with the frightful encounter, so simply on a hunch, I decided to learn more about what had formed my grandfather to become the man that he was. How had he become the rough, stern personality that had injured me as a boy? Hopefully, I could demystify this larger-than-life figure of my childhood.

(I sometimes find this method of investigation a way to humanize an abuser; that is, to appreciate their complexity and thus grow beyond a narrow and rigid black and white view of them and the world. However, as I show below, this approach may not be suitable for some people who have been victimized.)

Since my grandfather had died many years previously, I had to turn to my relatives to know his history. I discovered surprising details about his early life. He had suffered under the stern hand of his autocratic father, a man who my still-idealizing relatives described as someone who was "respected in the community" (but more likely feared for his authoritarian nature and financial power). I also learned that my great-grandfather was racist and had insisted that his son (my grandfather) violently "discipline" black workers on the family's turpentine farm in rural Alabama. Still in his late teens, my grandfather "punished the help" for their "negligence and laziness," an act that involved beating some men. Learning this helped me understand how my grandfather had turned against the tender, humane side of himself, thus making him capable of inflicting pain on me. According to one relative, my grandfather admitted to suffering recriminating guilt in his elder years for the racist acts he had committed.

There was more. I learned that my grandfather had inadvertently caused the accidental deaths of two of his children, for which he bitterly blamed himself, and which, in fact, nearly caused him to commit suicide as a result of his self-loathing. He and his oldest son had jacked up their car, attempting to repair it on their country dirt driveway which was not stable enough for the jack. The car fell and fractured the head of the first-born twenty-year-old underneath.

In another incident, my grandfather had thoughtlessly left a small can of flammable cleaning solvent on the fireplace mantel, and my mother, sixteen years old at the time, standing before the roaring fireplace one winter morning, reached up to see what was inside. When she turned the can towards her, the contents poured out, falling in front of my mother's six-year-old sister who stood beside her. The combustion of flames in front of the younger girl startled her, and she inhaled the heat, damaging her lungs. I am told that she died three days later while holding one of my grandfather's fingers in her tiny hand for comfort.

These deaths sorely afflicted my grandfather. On one occasion, my grandmother questioned him when she saw him returning from the woods, gun in hand, without game. He had been away from the house for an unusual amount of time, so she asked, "Where have you been?" He confessed, "I thought about killing myself."

But he did not. Fields needed plowing and planting, and there was a large family to raise. He did not abandon them. When I heard this part of my grandfather's story, I was touched. He became human to me.

My research gave me a fuller picture of the man that I had feared for much of my life, and as a result, I found the compassion that naturally arises when we understand the complex conditions that have formed someone to be who they are.

After realizing some of what my grandfather had suffered, I came to be impressed at how resilient he was. He had survived difficult times during the economic depression of the 1930s, even when immobilized by an illness that left him bedridden, unable to work for several months. He endured and found a way to provide for his large family on a farm in the rural south. He had not succumbed to suicide while suffering a near devastating depression following the loss of his two children and the painful realizations of the harm he had done.

Sometime after the dream of the monster pursuing me, having matured my understanding of my grandfather, he appeared again, but not as a demonic creature. In this dream, he was playing the piano and was filled with such enthusiasm and joy that he bounced up and down on the piano stool as he expressed delight. I was astounded that this man who had suffered near-suicidal depression, who had been harmed by his father, and subsequently had harmed others, could find his way to freedom. The hideous image of my grandfather had evolved, as they often do in dreams, and the once sinister dream figure had transformed and become an

inspiration to me as my grandfather played the piano exuberantly, a sure reminder that I, too, could come to terms with depressive moods and bouts of self-loathing that sometimes threatened to incapacitate me.

Other Ways of Working the Dream

My creative response to the monster dream was to cultivate a greater understanding of my grandfather. For others with such a dream, this might not be beneficial. Someone else might examine their personality to see if the critical grandfather is a picture of a harsh, demeaning trait within them, something that I could have certainly done. Someone else might rewrite the dream and show themselves turning and facing the approaching monster, then when close enough, look deeply into the menacing eyes, as frightening as that might be, and ask, "Who are you? Why do you wish to threaten me?" Much can be learned when sincerely posing questions to dream figures and waiting on their response. Then again, another person might simply turn and face the hideous figure and wait to see what would happen next, allowing the imagination to continue to extend the drama.

I did not mention that my monster dream was preceded by another dream that same night as if part one of two scenes. In the earlier dream, a hideous face also appeared before me, suspended in mid-air only a few feet away. I knew that if I ran, it would undoubtedly follow me. I thus concluded that it was my task to overcome my disgust and fear of the ugly creature by approaching it. In one of my rare acts of courage in a nightmare, I reached out with one fingertip and ever-so-lightly touched the face of the revolting figure. Immediately, it vanished.

In retrospect, it appears as if the first dream was preparing me to deal with the next, the one in which my grandfather pursued me. But as the second dream shows, I was not yet able to tolerate the confrontation with my grandfather. I awoke in a panic. Later, however, I did face him by investigating his history. By learning about the conditions that shaped him, my grandfather became humane to me. Consequently, I lost my fear of him.

Again, I am not proposing that my way of dealing with my grandfather is appropriate for others. Very often, someone victimized, especially in childhood by a parent, may already be too empathetic towards the abuser, prematurely forgiving them as a way to avoid their own legitimate but threatening anger. In such cases, the dreamer might be better served by revising their dream to show themselves standing up to an abuser, perhaps finally feeling and showing their legitimate, protective anger. For some, they may even confront the abuser with their abusive acts. In this way, a victim's dignity is strengthened.

There are no limits to the kinds of creative responses that we can make to a dream. The general rule of thumb, however, is to choose the one that satisfies you the most.

How the Shadow Comes to Help Us

If you follow your dreams closely, it is more usual than not to eventually encounter petty, rude, abusive, or self-indulgent characters, leading you to wonder, "How did they ever find their way into my sleep?" Additionally, you may very well come in contact with dream figures that are sick, troubled, and distressed, and your dreams may remind you of painful situations that you would rather forget.

Disturbing dream figures reveal shadowy parts of the personality—things about yourself that you would rather keep out of the light of awareness, hence known as *the shadow* in Carl Jung's psychology. Even though troubling, the advantage of discovering hidden things about yourself is that you can bring awareness to the forces in the personality that are undermining you. If left alone, they are likely to exert a troubling influence in your life.

An example of this is a woman who worked as a dietician in a weight loss clinic who dreamed of a large woman frantically "stuffing her face" with fast food.

The dreamer at first tried to minimize the dream's importance by assuming that she was just working too much. "Here I am," she thought, "doing overtime in my dreams." However, the woman's self-honesty made her realize that she didn't have the adverse reaction to her clients that she had to the desperate woman of her dream. She enjoyed the people she worked with, she said, and felt only warmth towards them. Her reaction to the dream figure, however, was one of disgust. This led the dreamer to consider that the hungry woman might be reflecting something within her rather than having anything to do with her clients.

As we explored the dream, the woman confessed a secret to me. After work, when driving home to her "empty house," she would stop at drive-by fast food stores, a behavior over which she felt shame. Because of her education, she knew that convenience food was bad for her, yet she felt an "irresistible urge" to buy highly sweetened shakes and fried foods. An athletic woman, she maintained her fit look through rigorous exercise, but she was troubled by her behavior because she knew the long-term health consequences of eating this way.

Using the dream as a mirror to see herself with greater clarity, the woman realized that she was attempting to stuff her troubling feelings down with "comfort foods," something that her mother had done for her when there was stress in the family. Rather than listen to her daughter, the overwhelmed, single working mother would buy fast foods to provide comfort for her children. "What we needed," she admitted, "was acknowledgment for the turmoil we all shared because of the financial distress we were in after the divorce. Just sitting and talking would have meant more to me than all the milkshakes and Buffalo wings we consumed."

As a result of the dream and her honest admission, the woman began reaching out to friends after work and consequently developed deeper bonds of closeness by revealing her heartfelt struggles rather than going it alone.

Shadow-work involves shedding light on that which is hidden, and because we hide that which we are ashamed of, shame is usually intensified when we admit to and reveal what is in the shadows. Therefore, a strong connection to compassion is needed to face things that we sometimes would not even want our best friends to know. But in addition to empathy, we need an insightful understanding of how the shadow comes initially to help us. For example, the dietician's fast-food compulsion comforted her. Even though it was not a final or sufficient solution, it did give her temporary relief from the social isolation she suffered. Understanding how the shadow is trying to solve a problem for us, despite its negative consequences, can help us explore our so-called bad habits and character deficits without the cumbersome and discouraging inner voice that simply punishes us for our weaknesses. Consequently, a compassionate attitude and awareness of how the shadow seeks to help us are far more helpful than willpower and self-castigation for our failures.

The figures of the unconscious are powerful and weak,
benevolent and insidious, and a very alert mind and heart
are needed to avoid the mass of possible traps into which
one can inadvertently step when dealing with them.
~ MARIE-LOUISE VON FRANZ IN ENCOUNTERS
WITH THE SOUL (HANNAH, 1981).

———————

Advocating for the Helpless

Some nightmares entail scenes of violence or exploitation. This is particularly true when someone has suffered trauma. In such cases, it is essential to not leave the dream in an unfinished state, one that lacks resolution. Nature seeks to elicit a life-affirming response from us through dreams, and if we depart from the dream, never re-envisioning it with a creative response, we leave a dream figure in a victimized, disempowered position. The personality is thus left in a fragmented state wherein one part (an aggressor) oppresses another (the victim).

It is essential to rewrite a dream narrative any time abuse occurs. This does not mean that your new version of a dream will bypass and make no mention of harm done. Instead, you benefit when creating a response to the reality of abuse, not denying or overlooking its truth. My strong advice when having suffered such a nightmare is this. Do not leave the victim alone and still suffering. Instead, step back into the dream in the revised version and intervene, acting as an advocate on behalf of the dream figure that was helpless and overcome by an oppressive force.

For example, in the original dream, a child may be overpowered by an abuser. In the revised version, you, the advocate, might enter the abusive scenario, stand in front of the abuser and firmly say "No!"

Intervening on behalf of a victim may require that you step into a new, unfamiliar role, one that is empowered, confident, and commanding. Here you can appreciate how important it is to Establish Safety inside yourself before you take such action, even if it is only in your imagination. Once you ground yourself in a confident, loving presence, you are better able to be creative in how you intervene. After blocking the abuser with your physical presence, you as the advocate might then kneel next to the child and reassure him or her that you are now with them and they are safe. You may feel inclined to hold the child (perhaps a symbol of your younger self) and provide comfort.

While such post-dream interventions may seem contrived, making imaginal revisions of tragic scenes can have far-reaching benefits. I have witnessed numerous instances in which someone harmed for years in their dreams suddenly stops the repetitious nightmares when they rewrite the dream to show the victim taking a proactive stance towards an aggressor. For example, a woman who had suffered intruder dreams for years finally put an end to them when she revised the role she had always occupied. Rather than trying to escape her own house, she waited for the intruder to appear in the revised dream and then demanded to know the man's intention. "You can no longer continue doing this," she commanded. "Now what do you want?" At that, the recurring nightmares went away. This is an example of fulfilling one of a nightmare's primary intentions: to move the dreamer out of a fight, flight, freeze strategy, and instigate a courageous, creative response.

I should mention here that Nightmare Completion is well suited for changing memories of waking life as well as dreams. Memories of real-life events need not be left as they were first formed. We can go back into them, insert ourselves as wise, protective advocates, and create an ending that gives honor and dignity to the helpless, injured, or oppressed. The following is a story of a woman who suffered painful, intrusive memories after accidentally driving her car into a young child who had darted out across the street while chasing a ball.

Intervening When Collapsed and Overwhelmed

A girl suddenly appeared, coming out from behind a parked car, giving no time for the woman to stop. For years afterward, Loretta, the driver and the mother of a child near the same age, dreamed of nightmarish scenes in which she would drive over or crash into items along the road, leading her to wake up in a panic. She would then be overcome with grief and shame as she recalled the actual death of the young girl she had hit. The dreams and the intrusive memories came unexpectedly day or night and caused Loretta to feel defeated as if she would never feel joy again, nor in her mind did she feel that she deserved to ever be happy after taking the life of another.

I advised Loretta that she could intervene in the reoccurring memory and treat it as an unfinished dream in need of a better ending. While I did not spell out how she might do this, I did encourage her to find a creative response to the tragedy that would enable her to live with the memory in a new way, one that did not constantly replay the tragic ending over and over.

To my surprise, Loretta introduced a scene that was sorely lacking in the original event. Here is her journal entry that describes the revised memory.

> Suddenly the girl appears. I feel the impact of her body before I can brake. I see her body thrown ahead of me. As happened in the actual incident, I'm able to swerve around her body as I come to a screeching halt. In an instant, I'm out of the car and rush to the girl, just like in real life. But when I touch her lifeless body, I'm overcome with dread. I fear that she's dead.

> I don't know what to do. I don't dare move her, since I fear hurting her more. I become paralyzed in shock and fear.

> Usually, this is where the memory stops.

> I recall more. I see the medics come and attend to the dear girl. I watch, just as I did, close by, but now I add a scene.

> As the medics start to take her away, I stop them and reach down and pick the precious little girl up in my arms—something I dared not do in actual life—and I hold her close and tell her how deeply grieved I am for ending her life prematurely. I ask her for forgiveness. Then I send love into her, and I intend for this love to go with the girl wherever she goes. I hold her like this as long as needed, and no one rushes me. I then lay her down on the gurney.

Rather than being in shock and turned in on myself, this time, I stand on my feet and watch the ambulance take her away. I continue to hold love for the precious little one in my heart to strengthen and console her for the new life that she, like me, must face.

Loretta's deeply genuine and heartfelt intervention moved her into a different role. Previously, she had been caught in relentless self-accusation, reviewing what else she could have done to prevent the accident. This singular focus caused her to feel helpless and overcome with regret and self-recrimination. But by realizing herself as an active agent of love, sending support to the girl as she entered an unknown future, Loretta transcended her helplessness and shame, no longer "turned in on" herself as she had been the day of the accident. Not surprisingly, the nightmares ceased, and just as relieving, the intrusive memories gradually receded as she practiced her creative intervention in the weeks that followed.

Intervening During a Rape

Another example of how the Nightmare Completion process can be applied to both dreams and waking life events comes in the story of Maria, a Guatemalan immigrant who came to the United States under great duress. Maria knew she was placing herself in harm's way when she dared to leave her country. She had heard many accounts of women who were raped in their quest to find safety in the United States, so she prepared herself with birth control and many prayers. But weighing the danger of remaining in Guatemala vs. leaving, there was no question which option would be the safest.

Maria had lost her husband when he was caught in the crossfire between warring gangs. While not on either side, his mere presence at the shootout caused each gang to suspect that he was allied with the other. By association, Maria was thus considered to be a collaborator. Fortuitously, she learned that her daughter, who was nearing puberty, was about to be taken as punishment for her husband's supposed disloyalty. Maria fled her home in the middle of the night after being alerted of her daughter's dire situation. However, she did not anticipate that her greatest danger lay north of the Mexican-US border.

After a grueling journey of several weeks, Maria arrived and was given temporary protected status. As she waited for her hearing to determine if she would be granted asylum, she found work as a domestic helper. There, she was raped by the "man of the house," an American-born retiree who lived alone. Fearful that she would not be believed and that her tenuous legal standing would be compromised, she quietly left her job, never pressing charges. She soon found employment elsewhere, but her ordeal was not over. It had just begun: Maria began suffering terrifying nightmares in addition to intrusive flashbacks of the rape.

I learned of Maria through a therapist I was mentoring in dreamwork, a woman who did volunteer counseling with Maria and others at a local women's shelter. After the therapist explained the nightmare completion process to Maria, she expected that it would require several more sessions before Maria would find the courage to "take the Crucial Step" and face her tormentor (in her imagination). But this was not the case. At the very next meeting, Maria returned with noticeable relief. She reported that indeed she had "completed business," having put an end to both her disturbing dreams and the intrusive memories of the rape.

Here is an edited summary of Maria's verbal account of her creative response.

> The memory, the flashback was always the same. It came out of nowhere during the day, and it always came whenever I had a nightmare that reminded me of the rape. In my dreams, I'm chased, and I get trapped on a dead-end street. I wake up in a panic. It's then that the memory comes.
>
> I usually only recall one part of what happened to me. It's when he's on me, holding me down. It's his breath I most remember and hate. It's hot, fast, and revolting. It's strange, isn't it? It's not the penetration that comes to mind, though I can recall it if I try. It's his breath that disgusts me. This is when I've always tried my best to get away from the memory and distract myself.

After our talk (with the therapist about nightmare completion), I stayed with the memory and waited for an idea that would bring an ending to this bad story.

I knew immediately what I wanted to do, but I didn't dare do it. I'm evangelical, Protestant, and we're warned against taking revenge. We're taught to turn the other cheek, just like Jesus did. I've tried forgiving that man. But it hasn't worked. I realized that if I were honest deep down, what I wanted to do instead was reach for his throat and, how do you say, "aplastar su tráquea" (crush his trachea). That's what I wanted to do.

You told me to trust my gut, my first impressions. Without this encouragement, I would've turned away and not done the bold thing. Here's my completed dream and memory.

He's lying on top of me. His breath repulses me. But I know from the years that I gripped a machete for splitting coconuts at the market that I'm capable of driving my fingers into his throat and grasping his, how do you say it, "windpipe?" So, just like what happened, he's holding both my arms down, and I know the only way to get free is to insult him, to spit in his face. That's what I do because I know he will slap me with his right hand, and that will free my left hand, my strongest, to grab his throat.

I cough up *esputo* (sputum) and forcefully spit into his face. I then turn my face to the right as he swings at me and misses me. At the same time, I remember exactly where his throat is, and I plunge my stiffened fingers deep into his neck and grab hold of his tráquea (trachea). He immediately takes hold of my left arm with both

hands, but my grip is firm, and the more he tries to pull my hand away, the greater his pain. I feel and hear the crunching of his *tráquer* as it collapses.

Maybe I shouldn't say this, but it's this sound and feeling of crushing his *tráquer* that satisfies me the most.

He coughs and gasps for air. I hold tight. Then his body surrenders.

I push him off me and over onto his back, still holding his throat with the strength of a *Tortuga toro* (snapping turtle). He looks at me, a frightened man. I look back, unafraid. He knows that he's lost. I let go, stand up, and feel the power of standing tall and strong above him. This time I don't run. I walk away.

Maria's surprising intervention worked, and it did so, I believe, because her creative response actualized dormant protective forces in her personality that she had suppressed at the time of the rape. Even after the assault, her strong religious proscriptions against any form of aggression ("turn the other cheek"} had undermined her instinct to protest the perpetration she had suffered. This all changed when Maria allowed her imagination to do what was needed to make her safe.

I was deeply inspired when I learned of Maria's courage to follow her genuine impulse. Her willingness to step into her aggressive, protective nature helped me appreciate the importance of allowing the imagination free rein to find the missing action necessary to resolve a nightmare or revise a painful memory.

Maria's example also helped me understand the troubling fantasies that took hold of me after an acquaintance had harmed me. Compared to what Maria had suffered, I had more or less only been inconvenienced, yet, like Maria, I had to trust an unfamiliar side of myself to find a resolution.

My Questionable Intervention

To help an acquaintance who had recently divorced and was having financial difficulty, I advanced money to her in exchange for her producing a few short educational videos. To my astonishment, the woman quit the project mid-stream and left the country with only a short note of explanation ("the amount of work was too much"). Rather than attempt to renegotiate the terms of our agreement, she simply took the money and ran, refusing communication.

I was left heartbroken because I had trusted the woman and had grown fond of her. But my grief soon turned to anger, and it would not leave me alone. I called and emailed, appealing for more communication, but she did not respond. I eventually wrote a piercing letter, but this did not leave me in any way satisfied.

I was surprised at the strength of my anger, and to my consternation, it only intensified over the next couple of weeks. I tried forgiving the woman. It did not work. I sought to better understand her and the complexities of what had led to our conflict, but this did nothing to give me relief. It was then that I decided to allow my feelings to do what they wanted. I gave them free rein to go where they desired (necessary for a creative response), and this led to me, quite surprisingly, fantasizing about puncturing the woman's tires. Yes, I began fantasizing about slashing her tires. The thought of the woman waking up, rushing out the door to teach her morning Pilates class and finding all four tires flat to the ground gave me immense pleasure. I must admit, however, that while satisfying, I also felt sheepish and judgemental towards myself for the fantasies.

The drama of this story came to a finale a few days later as I sat in Houston's Hobby airport during a layover as I traveled to vacation with friends in San Miguel de Allende (Mexico). During the wait, I must admit to becoming engrossed with online videos of people describing how they had slashed tires in response to feeling helpless and without a way to settle a grievance. I couldn't stop listening to the accounts, though I was embarrassed and even suspicious of where these fantasies were taking me. Yet, I knew that I was watching not only the videos but my imagination as well from a place of what in meditation is called "witness consciousness," meaning that I was not wholly consumed and taken over by the vengeful fantasies. I observed and considered them to be the expression of a robust protective force arising in me, so I allowed them.

After some time, I had had enough, and I checked my flight status only to learn that I had missed my connecting flight! I eventually arrived at my friends' Airbnb in San Miguel, feeling chagrined over my 11 pm arrival, five hours after we had agreed to meet for dinner.

My friends had kept the evening meal warm for me. As I sat down to eat, I described what had caused me to be late. When they heard my story, both psychologists with solid spiritual practices, they nearly rolled on the floor with laughter. "You were slashing tires in the Houston airport?" they asked, thoroughly entertained and without any judgment whatsoever. Suddenly the spell broke. I was over my anger. I had finally established justice in my imagination, and my friends' response dispelled my self-judgment about my fantasies. Consequently, I finally felt complete. Now I smile when I recall the entire incident.

In retrospect, I suspect that my revenge fantasies were attempting to counter my tendency to deny my grievances when hurt and overcome a propensity for being neglectful of my self-interests. I have noticed that since this incident happened, I now check myself when tempted to prematurely extend trust to someone before they have earned it. A needed cautiousness and discernment has been born in me that protects me from being naive.

One never knows what someone requires to finish a story. In both Maria's case and mine, as vastly different as they are in the severity of harm done, unconventional responses were crucial to finding a resolution. The spontaneous creative impulse that works may be in opposition to what someone judges to be moral or in good taste. When a revenge or setting-the-record-straight fantasy works, I believe it is because it activates dormant protective forces in the personality that have been denied. But for some, such fantasies may not lead to resolution and instead only result in unmediated toxic bitterness. Therefore, the defining question is, "Does your creative response bring a satisfying resolution to the inner conflict?"

My story, and perhaps Maria's as well, will cause some readers to feel alarmed. After all, doesn't violent behavior start with violent fantasies? The writer I have referred to several times in this book, Alice Miller, has helped me understand that it is actually when violent fantasies are suppressed and denied that they are more likely to be acted out in impulsive ways (Miller, 1980). However, when we provide an inner *container* for fantasies by establishing safety within ourselves—the first step in the nightmare completion process—and remain still, calm, and watch the creative process unfold in the way that it spontaneously desires, resolution can happen.

Many people fear giving such latitude to their imagination because of spiritual prohibitions or having learned early in life that an abuser would become even more hurtful if they express their anger. Thus, they pushed down their protective instincts. If such dampening of the instinctual animal remains, then a person is left vulnerable, unable to advocate on their behalf.

It is in the world of imagination that we can experiment and allow our protective instincts to mature. We can try out new behaviors, see how it feels, and refine our skills in fantasy.

In Maria's completion process, she found the missing piece, the side of her personality that was full of strength and enabled her to stand for herself. For others, an aggressive response may not be what's missing. Recall the story in the chapter *From Actor to Director*, in which Emily dreamed of all the people that had ever mistreated her. They were gathered at a house, ridiculing her, causing her to flee in terror. Emily's creative response (in her revised dream) was to stand her ground rather than run. She pictured herself stronger than her accusers. Unintimidated, she finally stood before each one and tolerated their criticism without succumbing to shame.

To complete a nightmare or a painful memory, we may have to experiment (in our imagination) before we find the very attitude, insight, or behavior that will bring resolution. A nightmare need not remain as it was when we first dreamed it, nor must a memory stay the same as when it was formed. Knowing this gives hope. When entered sincerely and soberly, the imagination can be a potent, restorative process that can enable us to go back into memories or dreams and change them. We do this not by attempting to erase the reality of a painful event by pretending that it never happened, but rather by augmenting our response; that is, by re-imagining ourselves as acting as a more creative, skillful, and empowered agent.

When a Dream Figure Is Too Weak to Act

You will note in the above examples that the dreamers were able to craft revisions that showed them acting with strength. In the first story, Emily initially dreamed of others ganging up on her to criticize her. Her creative response was to stand her ground and tolerate each person's harsh judgment without running away. In the second example, Loretta, the woman who had accidentally killed a child, chose to lift the body of the young girl up in her arms and send love into her rather than remain in a frozen state. Lastly, Maria imagined herself acting with the skill of a martial artist, stopping the man who was raping her by driving her fingers into his throat.

Unlike the above examples, some people may find themselves so incapacitated in their dream that they are unable to later imagine themselves acting with strength and courage. In such instances, the dreamer, once awake, may have to act on behalf of their weakened self. This was the case with Robert, a veteran I once knew who had repeated nightmares of being left on the battlefield in a dazed state as the result of an explosion that took part of his leg.

Robert could not revise his dream, which was practically a repeat of the actual event he had suffered. He felt no creative impulse to change or add anything new whatsoever to the dream. He could only see himself trapped in a dazed state, unable to move.

In speaking with Robert, I learned that he had essentially dropped out of life after his discharge from the military. He had withdrawn from friends and had no contact with anyone outside of work except for his wife. After having been an all-star high school athlete, a local celebrity actually, Robert felt that his life was over because of the amputation. The dream, which had repeated itself week after week for two years, appeared to me to be a diagnostic picture, like an x-ray, that was attempting to give Robert a truthful picture of his present dilemma. A big part of Robert did not want to wake up and face the emotional pain of being a man with a different body.

The turning point in Robert's nightmares and his life came when he reached into the dream to save himself. He extended his hand into the battle scene where he lay and grabbed the hand of the wounded, defeated soldier that he was. But to do this, Robert had to find enormous empathy for what he suffered and had lost that day on the battlefield. Rather than continue to withdraw from life in shame and defeat, he had to believe in himself again and infuse enough courage into his wounded self to return to the new life that was waiting for him.

The simple act of Robert finally grasping the hand of the defeated warrior that he was, moved me to tears, and it remains as one of the most courageous acts I have witnessed in dreamwork. It took an enormous effort for Robert to overcome the temptation to give up on life. But his one, singular act of grasping the hand of his defeated self proved to be decisive, yielding far-reaching benefits. You will read more of Robert's story and how he found his way to courage in the chapter *The Soldier Who Could Not Wake Up.*

4

Living the
New Dream

When I first started studying dreams some thirty years ago, I was focused on finding out what they meant. I was not content to be amused and entertained. I also wanted to understand dreams in hopes that they could help me live a more satisfying life. While my approach was noble and respectful of the intelligence that orchestrates dreams, little did I know that understanding alone is not sufficient to reap the full benefits that dreaming offers.

I was fortunate to find a therapist who helped me unravel the dream's mysterious and elusive meaning, but she did not stop there. After discovering a meaningful interpretation, she would deftly challenge me, often with razor's edge precision, to actualize the truth of the dream in daily life.

For example, sometimes I would tell my therapist a dream of a beautiful, attractive woman that caused my heart to fill with inspiration. After distilling the essence of the dream figure by naming the particular qualities that made the woman distinctive and unique, she would ask, "Can you now make love with the image, Len?" At first, I would startle inside, saying to myself, "What?!? Make love with the image? What on earth does she mean?" But it did not take me long to learn. It is not enough to know the meaning of a dream. To gain full value, you have to open yourself emotionally and viscerally to the qualities that a dream figure embodies and represents. In this way, you are changed by the image.

I once dreamed of a woman whom I intuited was a yoga teacher. She was not someone I knew. In fact, I did not even see her face. All that the dream showed me was the strong erector spinae muscles along each side of her spine. Upon awakening, I puzzled over the image and thought, "What on earth could this mean?" To explore the dream, I followed a guiding principle of dream investigation—*Distill the Essence*—and sought to name the essential *qualities* that made the dream image distinctive. This is what came to mind.

"Being a yoga teacher, she is flexible," I surmised. "And from the beautifully developed muscles along her spine, I know her to be strong. Putting these two qualities together," I determined, "the dream figure embodies a unique combination of *strength with flexibility.*"

In the days that followed, I kept the dream image and these qualities in mind. Consequently, I would catch myself slumping. I also noticed that my poor posture coincided with a feeling of slight discouragement, having fallen into an old pattern of living without confidence. As I breathed the yoga teacher's essence into my body, the capacity of being both strong and flexible, I felt myself immediately wanting to stand and sit taller, infused with the courage to approach whatever task before me with *gusto*—not a word I normally used, but that fit this new feeling that came to me. The image of the strong and flexible spine, once I embodied it, infused me with a subtle but certain zest and enthusiasm for life.

It may not be surprising for you to know that this dream came at a time when I was struggling with impediments to a new business. The dream helped me to be firm and persevering, but not only that, the flexible spine reminded me to be adaptable to the ever-changing conditions in the marketplace and thus not become willful and stubbornly push my way to inadequate solutions.

The above example demonstrates another guiding principle I often utilize when studying a dream: *Merge with the Essence.* The idea is that once you have found the meaning of a dream—for example, to be strong and flexible—the next step is to *breathe the image in*, as if you are letting it become a part of you, permeating every cell of your body. This *immersive bonding* with the image, feeling the distinctive qualities as if your own, is what my therapist had in mind when she asked me, "Can you make love with the image?" She used an erotic metaphor to signify how important it is to be fully immersed and viscerally affected when you remember a dream. In this way, valuable insights from a dream have a better chance of being assimilated and made a part of the personality.

The Warriors

There are many ways to become intimate with the truth of a dream. As described in the chapter Knowing Your Adversary, you will recall my dream of the primal African warriors who invaded my bedroom. In the weeks that followed this decisive encounter, I kept these men in mind as

I moved through my day, remembering their pointed spears for defending themselves and their readiness to follow their instincts. I observed by contrast whether I was living with a similar kind of primal masculinity. Recalling the bushmen in this way, I would catch myself when I would fall into old patterns of passivity, acquiescence, or overriding my gut feelings. As I imagined being like them, merging with their essence, I found that I became a more robust version of myself. Bearing the bushmen in mind, I checked myself more quickly when I was prone to go silent and not speak up for myself.

The bushmen burst into my life some twenty-five years ago, and I have remembered their instructive message hundreds, if not thousands of times. I have not only recalled the insights gained from them, but I have also *practiced feeling* what it is like *to be* them, that is, to embody the qualities that they inspired in me. With their pointed spears as inspiration, I determined to speak with greater precision and directness. Remembering how closely they lived in nature and stayed true to their instinct, I have found encouragement to honor my gut feelings. As a result, I have learned that tension in my abdomen is often a deep intuitive warning signal, attempting to give me caution lest I rush unwisely into a decision.

By holding the image of the bushmen close to me, new masculine potentials have been awakened and have become a stable part of my life.

As with the bushmen warriors, I have practiced merging with dream figures for many years, and this has been a crucial part of me growing into someone I never imagined I could be. Because of the rigid fundamentalism of my childhood, I was inflexible, shy, and accommodating to a fault. I did not know how to articulate my feelings, and I withdrew from relationships when there was conflict. Over the years, however, I have been mentored by so many dream figures that I have lost count, and they have helped me overcome my early deficits. In this regard, they have been some of my most influential teachers.

The Bear

You will recall my frightening dreams of the bear as described in *Knowing Your Adversary*. This dream image came to symbolize sovereignty for me, the capacity to govern and be true to oneself. Without this, we fall prey to equivocation and fail to live according to our deepest in-

stincts. I have dreamed of the bear at crucial moments in my life, and I now know that I need to trust myself more when it appears.

The last time I dreamed of the bear, I was vacationing with good friends I had not seen in at least a couple of years. After spending several days hiking, eating out, and going to the cinema, I felt a need to introvert and spend time writing. In fact, the vacation came when I had just started a new book, and creative ideas were flooding me. The muse wanted me to find time to record the inspiring insights I was receiving. However, since I had not seen my friends in a long time, and they were eager for all the socializing we could fit in, I felt awkward about saying what I wanted, so much so that I denied myself and went along with our extroverted activities. Unfortunately, this did not sit well with the muse in me, and I became withdrawn, preoccupied, and not fully present with my friends.

That night the bear came to me, and once again, I was frightened, indicating that I was not aligned with the power of sovereignty. Immediately I knew that I had failed to follow my instincts. I had fallen into an old, outdated version of myself that had learned to put the needs of others above my own, as was required in a home that demanded obedience to God and family.

As I lay awake in the middle of the night, musing on the bear's nature, I remembered that for us in North America, the bear is equivalent to the lion in Africa, King of the Jungle. I imagined how it would feel to know this same spirit of kingship within me, subservient to no one, living true to my deepest instincts. Immediately, I realized how I had failed to act with courage. Being fearful of offending or disappointing my friends, I had not even broached the subject of me taking time to write.

I shared my dilemma the next morning with my friends—I wanted to play, yet I needed solitude. Being gracious hosts, they gave me their full support and even arranged a desk with flowers in the gazebo in the back of their house among the trees. I spent a couple of productive days there—still enjoying great dinners with my friends at night. Some of the words in this book were written then.

Dream images are meant to be lived with, not just interpreted. If allowed to be an intimate part of our imagination, they can change our moods and behaviors and guide us. In this sense, I think of dream images as having psychoactive properties, just like an antidepressant or anti-anxiety medication. However, just like with any corrective medicine, we must do more than think about an image to have this effect. As my mentor encouraged me countless times, we must merge with an image to digest and absorb the qualities of a dream figure (like sovereignty, for example). In this way, we are changed.

Maria

In the previous chapter *Advocating for the Helpless*, I described how a Guatemalan refugee found unexpected satisfaction when she intervened on her behalf and created a different conclusion to the memory of her assault. She thrust her fingers into the throat of her perpetrator and crushed his trachea with her strong hands. Not only that, in her revised memory, Maria pushed her abuser off of her and then stood above him, holding him in her power, eye to eye as he lay helpless on his back. The revision to her haunting memory infused Maria with an *experience* of her protective powers, which had been suppressed for many years (out of necessity) in a highly patriarchal and violent culture.

With remarkably clever instincts for using the power of imagination, Maria kept reliving the ending of her revised memory, remembering what it was like to "stand on strong legs with feet planted in the ground," while looking down at her defeated abuser. She called on this crucial concluding scene whenever she felt weakened and intimidated by the lengthy and uncertain legal proceedings to determine her legal status. This proved  decisive for her when challenged in her final hearing. Standing confident and firm, Maria spoke persuasively and was granted permanent asylum.

The Power of Rehearsal

You may recall the great relief that nightmare sufferers found when using Image Rehearsal Therapy. As discussed in the chapter *Taking the Crucial Step*, researchers (Krakow and Zadra, 2010) found that an overwhelming majority of people who completed a six-hour program conducted over three weeks dramatically reduced the frequency of their nightmares. Not only that, the participants also reported less anxiety, depression, and symptoms of PTSD. The brief training consisted of learning basic relaxation skills (Establishing Safety) and then rewriting the narrative to have a different outcome (The Creative Response). For those who completed the training and continued to rehearse their revised dream for two to four weeks, 90% of them reported a dramatic (not just statistically significant) reduction in nightmare frequency.

Rehearsal of the revised dream is the last component of nightmare completion, but it is no less important than the other steps. In fact, repeatedly reviewing insights you have obtained from a dream and rehearsing your creative response to a nightmare is crucial if you want to derive what I have referred to as the "psychoactive" effects of a dream image. Through repeated remembering, new neural pathways are stabilized, and the wisdom and new skills learned are integrated into the personality.

Unfortunately, I have observed that even people who take their dreams seriously stop short of this critical process. Once an interpretation has been found, they move on and rarely reflect on the dream again. In my view, discovering a meaningful understanding of a dream is only the first step of a more extensive and rewarding process, sometimes referred to as dreamwork (as opposed to dream interpretation). As you will see below, it is possible to enter into a living relationship with dream images and derive similar benefits as you would when conversing with any wise teacher or sage.

Dream images are fleeting, even when they are nightmarish and riveting. The demands of waking life quickly crowd out the memory of a dream, and this is all the more so when we want to forget a so-called difficult dream. There is a reason for this. Dreams in general and nightmares, in particular, attempt to counter deep, habitual patterns of thinking and behavior that deprive us of a fully lived life. The fact that a dream is frightening indicates its unwelcome truth, even when its insight is good for us. Nightmares hold wisdom for us, but it is often inconvenient and challenging to our accustomed way of being. For this reason, even when we agree with the sobering message of a dream, we still need to make a special effort to keep its truth alive.

Three Ways to Deepen the Truth of Dreams

At the beginning of this chapter, I gave several examples of how other dreamers and I continued to live with dreams and thus reaped benefits beyond the initial revisioning or discovery of a meaningful interpretation. While knowing the meaning of a dream or revising a nightmare can be enlivening, there are benefits that can be experienced beyond this. I will now discuss three ways to actualize and extend the truth of a dream into everyday life.

- Remember a Dream with Feeling
- Ritualize the Truth of a Dream
- Honor the Dream's Ethical Demands

To illustrate how important these three components are, I will have you recall the story of Carl, whom you met in *Absorbing Difficult Truth*. His nightmares did not occur when he dreamed, but rather it was when he woke up from dreaming of his former lover that he was overcome with inconsolable grief. As you may remember, Carl was a classic alpha male who had become accustomed to blustering and bullying his way through life. Not only was he a big man physically, but he was also loud and demanding. To Carl's way of thinking, his bravado had rewarded him with success. In his words, his "strong leadership" (which appeared to me to be heavy-handed) had enabled him to grow a fledgling start-up into a robust business. But when his girlfriend departed, none of his usual methods of "assertive persuasion" brought her back, nor did his aggressive manner enable him to find consolation for his overwhelming sorrow.

Carl attempted to assuage his pain by having a series of affairs. But the woman he still loved would appear in his dreams. This brief but potent contact with her opened the portals of denied grief upon awakening, making it impossible for him to concentrate at work for hours afterward.

There are many reasons why we dream of someone we have lost. The popular understanding is that this is simply the normal process of "working through grief." Another explanation is that dreams of the departed are wish-fulfillments, an idea from Freud which asserts that we dream to satisfy what we wish for but can no longer have in reality. After having listened to a great many dreams about departed loved ones, through death or separation, I think something far more substantial is occurring. Often the dreamer needs to make peace with the departed by facing up to unfinished business, acknowledging regrets, or drawing inspiration from the loved one for the new life they face alone. Said another way, when someone continues to dream of the departed, they are likely attempting to understand what the person *means* to them. In fact, the search for *meaning* is now thought to be a sixth stage in the traditional five stages of grief developed by Elizabeth Kubler-Ross (Kessler, 2019).

While not intending to take issue with any of the above ideas, I wish to add another possibility: I believe the dream may use the presence of someone we miss and long for to initiate a profoundly intimate change in us. The one who visits us in our waking fantasy or dreams at night may very well possess and exemplify those qualities we need to cultivate within ourselves.

I have personally experienced how my dreams have used the presence of someone I loved and missed to bring about psychological and spiritual shifts in my personality. It is my experience that when we long for another, there are vital characteristics in them that we need to actualize within ourselves. Until this is accomplished, we may yearn for them intensely, continue to grieve for them long after they have departed, and only "get over them" when we have assimilated and actualized their enviable qualities within us. Those who have gone through this most intimate process know that you are not left the same. While at times an arduous undertaking, your personality is expanded and deepened because, in one sense, you have taken the other into yourself and become more like the one you have lost. But to accomplish this, you must see beyond the person you miss and ask, "What is it *about them* that I must come to terms with?"

As I listened to Carl's disruptive dreams of his former lover, I sensed that more was involved than his attempting to "get over her." I suspected that he needed to integrate the woman's presence into his personality, cultivating in himself the qualities that he adored in her. If I were to help Carl accomplish this, however, I had to help him identify the qualities his girlfriend possessed, the characteristics that drew him to her. Otherwise, he would continue to long for a reunion with the woman literally and thus overlook the underlying qualities that were essential for him to incorporate into his life.

When I asked for details about the woman, Carl could not name what it was about her that moved him, which is often the case when we are so involved with someone that we cannot see them objectively. I asked Carl to tell me more about the dream. All that he could do was shrug his shoulders and say, "She was just being herself."

You may recall that after some probing, I suspected that it was the woman's humility that touched Carl, a missing but needful quality in his blusterous, domineering personality. Once identified as an attribute that he sorely lacked, Carl faced the tedious task of developing in himself this very quality that he found compelling in his former lover.

I continue Carl's story below because it illustrates how beneficial it is to *stay with the images of our dreams* long after we have interpreted or revised them. Substantial growth in the personality is accomplished not merely by understanding or revising a dream. We must *live* its truth and allow it to affect us in the days and weeks that follow.

As you will see below, Carl did this in three ways: he remembered his dream woman with feelings. He ritualized her. He honored the ethical mandate of his dream.

Remember with Feeling

There's nothing more effective for keeping the truth of a dream alive than letting yourself be fully absorbed when you recall your dream. When you remember a meaningful interpretation or recall your new role in the revised version (in which you are no longer a threatened victim), it is vital to do more than just think about the dream. If you allow yourself to be so fully immersed that you feel the truth of a dream in your body, you are more likely to assimilate (integrate) the potential of a dream and thus enrich the quality of your life.

As I sat with Carl, he spoke of a quality closely related to his lover's humility. He affectionately said of her, "She's so, so sweet." I invited Carl to imagine what it would feel like to have this same *sweet* humility living inside him. "If you allowed yourself to be this same way, how would it affect you? The way you walk; how you talk, both in and outside of work?"

Carl was baffled by this idea. Therefore, by contrast, I reminded Carl how he had pushed his way into my office the day we met. I asked if he would give me permission to switch roles and demonstrate how I remembered him. To my surprise, he agreed.

Pretending to be him, I went outside my office and banged on the door as he had done in our first meeting. When he answered, I gripped his hand firmly to show my dominance and then stiff-armed him to push him away at a safe distance. I then rushed in to take a seat, bumping into the coffee table to simulate how he had spilled his hot coffee that day. I then reminded him how loudly he had first spoken, causing me to ask that he lower his voice to respect my office mates.

Fortunately, Carl was thick-skinned enough, or perhaps so desperate for help, that he did not flinch away from my directness. He sat quietly without objection to my portrayal of him, perhaps seeing himself objectively for the first time.

I then spoke in a tender tone, "Of course you miss this woman. Her gentle, humble spirit disarms you. Judging by your dreams of her, you might even say that her feminine presence is pursuing you, seeking to remind you of something precious."

Knowing the breath to be the simplest and most intimate way of merging with the essence of a dream figure, I invited Carl to imagine breathing in the feeling of sweet humility. "While you breathe fuller and slower than usual, also imagine that you're allowing her gentle nature to come inside you. As Carl did so, his entire countenance relaxed.

"I feel quieter," he admitted.

"Yeah, I see. Your whole body let go." Knowing that Carl suffered from hyper-tension, I added, "Breathing these qualities into you would also be good for your heart. But..." I made a long pause to get his full attention. "You would have to do this dozens of times a day."

Carl was understandably puzzled.

"I suspect that you are continuing to dream of this woman because something wants to change in you. But the dream is having to work against a lot of old habits and ways of living that are antithetical to this sweet, unpretentious, self-accepting manner that your former lover embodies. You have to make room for her spirit to live in you."

Knowing that such ideas were verging on the esoteric for Carl, I asked, "How about we rewrite the scene of you rushing into my office the first day we met? Would you come in again and greet me, only this time allow this woman's presence to be inside you and affect the way you move?"

Carl was a risk-taker, and he did not shy away. Remarkably, even before he made his way outside, his entire manner had already shifted. He stood up slowly, walked quietly to the door, and opened it, barely making a sound. Without rushing, he stepped outside and re-entered my office as a different man. Whereas Carl's movement before had been chaotic, frantic, and loud, I was impressed how such a large man could now move so smoothly. He was surprised, too. He sat quietly taking in the change that had suddenly occurred. It may have been the first time Carl had felt what it was like to be calmly settled inside himself, just like the woman he so adored.

Of course, such changes are fleeting, at least in the beginning when the body and personality are conditioned to live in a more restrictive way. For this reason, brief body-embodiment practices like Carl did—breathing in the sincere, humble presence of his former love and then moving as if she were in his body—must be repeated many times. Additionally, if we imbue such practices with elevated meaning, as will be discussed below, we supercharge the simplest of gestures, like movement and breath, and potentiate a dream figure's capacity to evolve us into a newer version of ourselves.

Ritualizing the Truth of a Dream

Ritualizing a dream figure elevates its importance and thus enhances its capacity to enrich us. The most fundamental way of doing this is how we think of and name something or someone who appears in our dreams. Carl, for example, initially thought of the woman who came to him in his dreams as his girlfriend, his ex. And as in his story thus far, I have referred to her as Carl's *former lover/ partner*. However, as Carl would discover, the person of our dreams is not the same as the one in waking life.

If you are to derive the benefits of the dream's intelligence, you must eventually see a dream figure symbolically. In Carl's case, he came to see the woman of his dreams as representing qualities he needed to assimilate into his personality. But even here, a dream figure will likely remain an image, a mere symbol, something inert. Consequently, it will lack the emotional force needed to overcome and change patterns of thought and behavior limiting us.

At some point in our conversations Carl and I felt awkward about continuing to refer to the woman of his dreams as his former love, because in fact, she was not. This became clear to Carl when he reached out to his ex several times, hoping for a reunion. When his efforts miserably failed, he started questioning the dream woman's identity. "If she's not my ex, then who is she?" he asked.

I suggested the term "inner lover," which did not sit well with Carl. Though the designation works well for some, it was "too romantic" for him. He found a better description: his "inner woman," an identification that elevated her beyond just being a dream symbol to a real, living presence inside of him, capable of affecting and advising him if he listened.

In our culture, we essentially think of dream figures as inanimate figments of the imagination without any inherent life of their own. I often remember Carl Jung's words contradicting this notion.

> . . . there are things in the psyche which I do not produce but which produce themselves and have their own life (Jung, 1989, p.183).

When we relate to a dream figure as if it is *real*, autonomous, and alive, not just something imaginary, we ritualize the image and elevate its importance and thus its ability to affect us. Let me give an example of how this is done every day throughout the world.

In much of Christianity, a simple ritual is enacted each week. Christians eat a small wafer and take a sip of wine (for some, grape juice). For them, the bread and wine are symbolic of the "body and blood" of Christ, thus rendering a most common gesture, eating and drinking, into something sacred.

In like manner, if we relate to dream figures, especially those that inspire us, as real and intentional (purposeful) living *presences* that are capable of guiding us, then we will more likely treat them with respect, and thus listen to them and not forget them, as we usually do with dreams.

A tried and tested way to treat dream presences respectfully is to record what they do and say as if their actions and words are of value. This is best done by keeping a private dream journal. It is for no one else to read. If you choose to show what is in your journey, which may have drawings and pictures you have pasted inside, you do so selectively, as if sharing an intimate part of yourself. Note the importance that Carl Jung gave to the dream journal.

> You can go to the (dream journal) book, turn over the pages, and for you, it will be your church—your cathedral—the silent places of your spirit where you will find renewal...for in that book is your soul (Dunn, 2015).

I have kept dream journals for decades, and I believe this practice is one reason I have been able to find great wisdom in the dreaming process. As a result of recording my dreams, I have found it easier to remember them. Many people notice this reciprocal relationship between consciousness and the unconscious—the more we pay attention to dreams, the more they communicate with us. Also, by recording my dreams, I strengthened my capacity to be an astute observer of my inner world, which is one of the great benefits of keeping a journal.

These days I record my dreams with my laptop. To enrich the experience, I often search for images that illustrate what I have dreamed and then paste them into the text. There are times when I print an image and post it in a prominent place in my home so that I encounter it several times a day. Whenever I pass the image, I pause and remember the dream's significance, allowing it to affect me.

Some years ago, during a challenging period of my life, I felt a need for greater internal guidance. Therefore, I dedicated an entire wall of my home office to my dreams. I printed images I found on the internet that illustrated my dreams, and I would sometimes draw or paint dream figures and then post them on the wall that was directly opposite my desk. As a result, I would frequently look up and see reminders of insights that had come to me through dreams. By giving concrete expression to the subtle, imaginal world, I kept the truth of my dreams alive. As a result, the dream's intelligence was able to work on me more deeply. When we elevate dreams by giving them special importance, their powers are potentiated.

I have a friend who writes short, concise poems, much like Japanese Haiku, in response to her dreams. The process enables her to clarify and express what she describes as "the truth-essence" of her dreams. In this way, she works with the imagery so that, in her words, it is "digestible, useful, and long-remembered."

Here you might ask, "Why is it advantageous that we extend the memory of a dream, or in my friend's words, to make it "long-remembered"? To answer this, consider the task of evolution. It is to keep us adapted for the ever-changing challenges of life on earth. In my paraphrase inspired by the work of Charles Darwin, "It is not the strongest and fittest who survive. Rather, the future belongs to those who adapt."

Adaptation requires change. To use a computer metaphor again, outdated programs must be upgraded to remain viable and robust. When it comes to the human personality, this is not an easy process to undergo, for it necessitates that we let go of habitual ways of believing and behaving that no longer allow our fuller potential to be expressed. We humans are inclined towards safety, familiarity, and predictability, and from an evolutionary perspective, there is the danger of becoming fixed and inflexible.

Carl was caught between the man he had become—blustering, blunt, and entitled—and another version of himself of which he had only a vague idea. The disturbing dreams of his inner woman insisted that he evolve into a fuller human being. But this required that he develop qualities that appeared to be in opposition to all that had made him safe and successful. His dreams showed him another possibility. A tender side of himself was available, characterized by humility rather than arrogance. Like his inner woman, he might learn to show consideration for others rather than act with entitlement. But were it not for the dream's disturbing intrusion, Carl would have shown no interest in changing. Why would he? Life had seemingly gone his way until he suffered heartache.

Carl's inner woman reminded him of what he could be. Like a north star, which dream images often are, the calm, unpretentious presence of his dream woman pointed Carl to another man he might become. As Carl legitimized the woman of his dreams and treated her as a real presence, he began to listen to her more carefully. This led to an unexpected challenge from her.

Honor the Ethical Demands of a Dream

As mentioned above, when I began seriously studying my dreams, I was eager to know their meaning. Like reading a mysterious fable or fairy tale, I sought to understand the metaphor to obtain wisdom for living a more satisfying life. Never did I imagine that dreams would require anything from me.

Carl held similar ideas when he first came to me. In his mind, his disturbing dreams would stop if he could understand them; then, his life could return to normal. But as he would soon learn, "normal" was not the intention of his dreams. In fact, they seemed intent on disrupting the way he was living his life. His dreams were pushing him from within to grow into someone he had never been. Of course, this is what dreams do. They intend to evolve us, and they accomplish this by placing demands on us.

In the course of self-development and learning to be true to oneself, it is easy to assume that a self-actualized person gets to do whatever they wish. But, in truth, if you seek to actualize the many potentials within you, then you may be required to make what at first feels like a sacrifice. Familiar but outdated habits of mind and body have to be relinquished, including indulgences and self-absorption that block the newer, wiser, and more robust version of you.

The ethical imperative of Carl's dreams came in the most unsuspecting way. He dreamed of his inner woman, but this time she did not remain a few feet away as she usually would. Instead, she approached Carl, and not only that, she was fully naked. She reached and pulled Carl's cheek towards her lips, but before the kiss could be completed, Carl reached for her breasts, eager for intimate contact. The inner woman quickly brushed his hands away, though gently, not shunning or shaming him, but she made it clear that she was not there for the erotic. Carl followed her lead, gently embracing her waist instead. As he did, she kissed his cheek with such tenderness that Carl's heart was penetrated, opening him to a depth of love he had never tasted. In his words, "It was the sweetest kiss I've ever known."

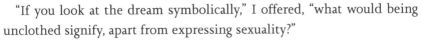

Carl was deeply moved afterward. Normally he would be thrown into inconsolable grief, but now he was unexpectedly calmed. "I swear it happened," he said, surprised by the hyper-realism of the encounter. "It was as if she was really there."

"Of course, she was," I confirmed.

Carl then posed a crucial question: "If she did not want sex, why did she come in the nude?"

"If you look at the dream symbolically," I offered, "what would being unclothed signify, apart from expressing sexuality?"

"You have nothing to hide."

"Yeah. Open and transparent. What would that mean for you?" I asked.

Carl paused, considering the question. After a long silence, he took an unusually deep breath and let it out forcefully as if having come upon something difficult and important. He uttered a big "Shit!" that silenced the room. I had the sense that Carl had been caught by something.

In previous weeks I had reviewed the various encounters Carl would have in a day, asking what his inner woman thought of his behavior. "How would she feel about the way you treated your staff today?" Or "What would she think about how you interacted with the mechanic who didn't fix your car on time?" Carl could be refreshingly honest, admitting when he was "an ass" and "in need of more patience." But the dream of his transparent woman wanted a deeper accounting.

Carl's big "Shit!" had to do with not wanting to give up his entitlement to date as many women as he wanted while pretending with each that she was the only one. For Carl to be aligned with his inner guiding presence, he had to show honesty, sincerity and not indulge the old self who knew how to get what he wanted through omission and pretension.

As you might imagine, the ethical demand of Carl's dream brought him into deep conflict within himself. He had built his entire life and career on the opposite of what his inner woman wanted. He never revealed his hand. He was strategic and transactional in all his relationships.

Carl could have easily dismissed the dream as wish fulfillment, the result of trying to live out a sexual or reunion fantasy. Fortunately, he did not do this. He could not discount the sobering truth of his dream. Following "the tenderest kiss he had ever known," he was assaulted (my words, not his) by dreams of being in a strange, unfamiliar city, separated from his inner woman. Desperate to locate her, he could not find his way out of a labyrinth of streets that kept bringing him back to the same spot.

Carl would wake from these nightmares perplexed and agitated. "What on earth do these dreams have to do with anything?" he protested.

"What if they were trying to help you, Carl?" I offered, hoping to arouse curiosity in what he otherwise felt was persecuting him.

"With what?" he gruffly asked.

"To help you find your way, of course. What truth is there in your labyrinth dreams? Are you going in circles? Are you living in such a way that you are separated from your tender, soulful nature?"

The dreams had a chilling, sobering effect on Carl, just as they intended. With the "tenderest kiss" dream as a backdrop, Carl's "lost and separated dreams" were all the more difficult to bear. Therein is the value of nightmares. They disturb us, shaking us out of our lethargy, our habituated way of living, and in this way, our evolutionary mandate has a chance of being fulfilled.

A great quote by Carl Jung often comes to mind when I find myself grumbling over the conflicts I feel inside myself.

> Nothing so promotes the growth of consciousness as this inner confrontation of opposites (Jung, 1989, p, 345).

It is when we are torn between opposing forces in our personality that something new can evolve.

Carl's inner mandate was no easy task. Over the next several months, he was brought into an intense confrontation between his old, familiar self, which was inexorably drawn to dominance, and the gentle but incisive voice of his inner woman that asked him to find his way into his heart.

I was impressed with how stealthy Carl's dreams were. In one sense, they were not expressly confrontational. They did not hit him over the head and accuse him of womanizing, narcissism, and deceit, though the dream is certainly capable of such. Instead, dreaming intelligence found a chink in Carl's armor, the place where he was defenseless. Once his heart was touched, he began to be disarmed from inside himself.

"Have you told any of the women you date about your story?" I asked one day. "Do any of them know what you're going through, that you still have heartache?" Carl looked at me with a blank stare as if he could not even conceive of this level of vulnerability.

"I suspect you're more in need of emotional intimacy than sex per se, Carl. Does it not leave you lonely, being a stranger to the women you are sleeping with? You could have much more than what you're getting. Your transparent woman is showing you how."

My challenge and indeed Carl's dreams led to him tentatively opening his life to his women friends. Not all at once, but gradually he began testing the waters, staying close to sincerity, genuineness, and unpretentiousness. It was not easy. But eventually, sex without intimacy became less satisfying. If Carl resisted this change, his dreams became upsetting. He would often wake up in a panic, having dreamed that his inner woman had left him. Such dreams reoriented Carl to the task before him: he must be true to a new way of being and behaving, characterized by living from his heart, no longer succumbing to the old forms of power and dominance.

Carl's story exemplifies one of the core features of nightmares: they intend to disturb us, to shake us out of fixed and restrictive modes of being so that something new can evolve in us. The capacity to bear such disturbance and understand what is called for is essential if we are to benefit from the evolutionary intelligence of difficult dreams.

Carl's dreams had an undermining effect on him. He could not go about his old life anymore, at least not without suffering heightened conflict within himself. As a result, his compulsion to be with as many women as possible gradually diminished. For some time, Carl even found himself unexpectedly celibate. It was the first time in his life that he could use solitude to become intimate with himself.

During this period, Carl slept by himself, but he was not alone at night. Though his inner woman visited him less, as a result of following her mandate, others took her place, each one asking something of Carl. When he said Yes and gave the Muse what she wanted, another piece of the old ornery Carl fell away.

———————————

I took great care to try to understand every single image . . . and, above all, to realize them in actual life. That is what we usually neglect to do. We allow the images to rise up, and maybe we wonder about them, but that is all. We do not take the trouble to understand them, let alone draw ethical conclusions from them... It is equally a grave mistake to think that it is enough to gain some understanding of the images and that knowledge can here make a halt. Insight into them must be converted into an ethical obligation...The images of the unconscious place a great responsibility upon a man. Failure to understand them, or a shirking of ethical responsibility, deprives him of his wholeness and imposes a painful fragmentariness on his life.
CARL JUNG (1989, P.192-193)

Dream
Stories

M ost books about dreams give at best a brief description of the person whose dream is described. Maybe their age, gender, and marital status are revealed, but little beyond that is discussed. It is rare to read about a dreamer's real-life situation and the anguish that gave rise to someone's nightmare. Such superficial treatment of dreams has always left me dissatisfied.

Even here in my book thus far, I have only given synopses of what led to someone's dreams, and I have provided just a snippet or two of the actual conversation that flowed between a dreamer and me. But now I wish to change that. In the following three stories, I give fuller accounts of how dreams can be listened to and how rewarding they can be if reflected on over a lifetime.

As you know by now, I do not depend upon predetermined and generalized interpretations found in dream dictionaries. Dreams are profoundly intimate experiences, and each one contains our unique fingerprint. A dream is thus deserving of an unbiased, respectful consideration, as much as an individual is, regardless of their gender, race, or cultural origin. For this reason, the first thing I do when I approach a dream is to listen to it without prejudice and then begin to investigate it with curiosity. Most often, I do this without having any idea initially about what a dream means.

When I first adopted this attitude as a psychologist, I was relieved. I no longer felt the pressure to show my competence by immediately interpreting someone's dream.

I hope the following three dream stories will show how rewarding it is to approach dreams this way. Also, by devoting an entire chapter to one dream each, I hope to convey how richly layered dreams are and that they are tied to the very fabric of our lives. They are not passing, ephemeral scenes haphazardly thrown together by random firings of the brain. If we listen skillfully, our dreams can reveal our most profound longings and fears.

The first story, *The Soldier Who Could Not Wake Up*, will be familiar to you because I mentioned it in a previous chapter when I described how courageous a young disabled soldier was when facing a recurring nightmare that plagued him after returning from war. This longer version of the story displays how earnest the soldier was and how courageous and compassionate we also must be to find the life-changing wisdom that a nightmare can bring.

The second story is my own. *The Witch I Finally Faced* illustrates how some of our earliest remembered dreams can shed light on the dilemmas we faced in childhood, but they can also reveal the challenges we will face as adults. In my case, I describe a dream I had at age five when I was chased by a terrifying witch. This dream has proven to contain some of the richest wisdom of my life, yet it took me several decades to appreciate and unearth the depth of information that it contained.

The third dream story, *Why the Serpent Chased My Mother*, describes how I came to understand my mother's recurring nightmare, mentioned in chapter one. Here is another dream that took me a long time to fully appreciate. This story demonstrates the rewards of staying with a dream over time and probing its depth.

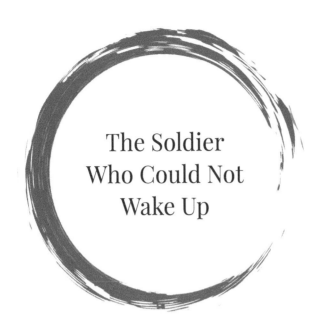

The Soldier
Who Could Not
Wake Up

The following story demonstrates how it is possible to interrupt years of frightful dreams with one singular act of intervening for a disempowered dream figure. Earlier in the chapter, *Advocating for the Helpless*, I introduced Robert, a wounded veteran who repeatedly dreamed of being dazed and unable to move after an explosion on the battlefield. His story illustrates how vital it is to be an advocate for weakened dream figures since they are often symbolic of aspects of ourselves. Here I provide a fuller account of how Robert found the necessary empathy to extend kindness to himself.

Robert came to me reluctantly and only because his wife insisted that he must do so. His disturbing dreams, and the sleep deprivation that followed, were a problem not only for him but for his wife as well. "Her nerves are running thin," he explained.

Robert was a strong, athletic-looking man in his late twenties, though he walked with an unexpected unevenness in his gait. Sparsely spoken, he held his jaws tight, and despite the attention he gave his gym-sculpted physique, he seemed not at home in his body. He was restrained and lacked expression on his face.

What follows are portions of two conversations I had with Robert in which he spoke of having a recurrent nightmare since returning from war.

> I basically have one dream, repeated a hundred different ways, but there are a few things that are always the same. There's been an explosion. I've been knocked out, but I'm coming back. I'm numb. Some senses are returning: ringing in my ears, muffled shouting, the smell of explosives. A haze of smoke blocks my vision. Then the sickening feeling: I can't move.

Robert pauses and studies my face, appearing to look for any indication that I am uneasy. He continues.

> In the dream I don't feel pain yet, but I know I've lost my leg, below the knee. I think to myself, "Your life's over, man. It ain't never going to be the same."

I asked, "What do you make of the dream?"

> There's no meaning. It's life as it happened in the war, but unlike life, it keeps repeating itself over and over. What do you do with a dream when there's nothing to interpret? Everything is real.

"It sounds like the kind of dream that doesn't need an interpretation. Only completion," I offered. My response was unexpected, and Robert paused to consider my words.

Completion? What does that mean?

"From what I see, it appears that your dreams are asking for a response from you. You need to act, to do something about the man's dilemma?"

What dilemma?

"He—you—can't get back into life. He's stuck there. Regardless of how many times you dream this, the scene always ends the same, right? He's dazed, in shock. How long has this gone on?"

Seven years.

"That's a long time to be in that state. A lot of life missed out on."

Again, another long pause. Not fully understanding all that I was intending, Robert shifts the conversation to waking life.

My wife tells me that I'm not like before, that I'm on edge, not affectionate. She worries about me. She says I mostly hang out alone, but I'm not bothered.

"Do you think you've changed?" He looks out the window. An awkward silence follows. No response.

As we talked more about life since the war, I realized that Robert could likely be diagnosed with PTSD, his nightmares, of course, being a key feature. He had withdrawn from life after returning from war, isolating himself into a protective shell. Before the military, Robert had a large group of friends, mostly centered around sports in which he had excelled. In fact, he had been something of a celebrity because of his athletic ability. But the injury in Afghanistan had snatched that from him.

Robert had joined the military in pursuit of respect and honor, not to mention financial gain. Yet, the medals earned, and the money made paled in comparison to the sacrifice he had given. Like many wounded warriors, he had returned disillusioned.

Robert struck me as disciplined, conscientious, and painfully isolated. Other than his wife, he spent time with no one outside of work.

"Your dream ends truthfully," I said. "Your life *did* end, the one you knew. It's never been the same. But there are other lives to be lived, Robert. But only if you can wake him out of his trance."

Who do you mean?

"The one you left on the battlefield."

What trance?

"You're always half-awake when the dream ends. Without all of your feelings. Is that how it is outside the dream as well?"

Silence. Robert looks outside again. I may have stepped over his comfort zone. But maybe he will respect my directness.

"I doubt if your dream is just a replay of war," I proposed. "For what good would that be? Have you considered that it keeps playing because the dream needs you? To finish the story?"

Silence again. Robert looks away but is contemplating, still engaged. I know I've led him into uncharted terrain. I sense that I need to lay out the big picture and give an idea of where we are headed.

"Did you know that you can go back into the dream, once awake, and pick up right where it left off?"

Oh, you mean lucid dreaming?

"No, I mean while you're awake, even right here."

I explained the idea of being an advocate; how we can re-enter a dream and help a dream figure who is weak. "It's like re-writing the dream, giving a different ending that doesn't end tragically. Of course, something tragic did happen, and you can't deny that; but you can do something in response to the tragedy. The important thing is that you don't just wake up and go about your day and leave your younger self alone in that dream."

Robert responded with a tone of sarcasm. "You mean just make up another ending, like that?" He was skeptical. Understandably so. No sleight of hand would erase his suffering.

"It's not just any ending. It's gotta' feel truthful, honest. We're not making up fantasy and pretending that your life didn't get torn apart. Your response has got to be gutty, something that makes a difference to that man in your dream."

Robert sat up in his chair, attentive.

"You can step right back into the scene, the memory of it—the haze in the air, the smells, and noise. You would be returning to that young man that you were when he had the life shocked out of him. What does he need from you, Robert, to help him out of his dilemma?"

Robert shifts in his chair, understandably tense about the idea. I clarify.

"You had the medic nearby. He took care of your body. You recovered, even if in a different form. But it's your soul that I worry about: that half-alive state that haunts you every time you dream it. I suspect that you're seeing something about yourself when you dream this; not just reliving what happened in Afghanistan."

Normally I would move slower, ask more questions to engage someone, but it was apparent Robert kept things to himself, revealing as little as possible. Perhaps he would respond better to information, so I sketched out a game-plan about what could happen if he signed on.

"Look, I understand. It's uncomfortable when you come across a dream that's like a mirror, reflecting something true back to you. It can be unnerving, especially if you don't know what you can do.

"But you can do something. The dream is waiting for you to take action. To help that man that you were when you got lost back then. He had the life shocked out of him, and he doesn't know how to get it back."

It was at this point that Robert tentatively joined me. He gave the slightest nod yes, a gesture I would have missed if I were not giving him my full attention. I also saw it when his face softened, his tight jaw relaxing, showing a sign of relief, I suspected, because he was no longer alone.

I explained how he didn't have to wait for the dream to play again at night. I showed him how to become still, breathe in a way that gives him pleasure, and then re-enter the dream.

"But you've got to do this carefully. You can't just rush in. You've got to take your time to get quiet inside yourself —and this may be the most difficult—you've got to learn how to calm yourself when you approach your dream. I'm talking about once you're awake and you decide to go back into the memory of it. What do you normally do as soon as you wake up from the dream?

I get up; turn the TV on, open the fridge. You know, anything.

"To distract. I get it. But now you've got to take a different approach. You've got to *stay* with the dream so that you don't turn away and leave yourself stuck once again in that dazed state.

Robert leaned forward, pensive, elbows resting on both legs, hands grasped tightly.

That's a lot, man.

"Look, have you ever been to the zoo? I remember once when I was five, my parents took me to a really nice one. There was a gorilla there, huge, fully grown, and of course much bigger than me. A thick glass partition separated us. I stood there looking at him when our eyes met. He was about twenty-five feet away, but he crawled off his perch and sauntered over towards my family. I became frightened, of course, and started backing away as it got closer. But my dad put his hand on my shoulder and reassured me. 'You're safe son. Just hold still.' And that's what I did. Wouldn't you know it? The huge beast came right up to me and sat down on the other side of the glass.

"The gorilla wasn't more than three feet away from me, and we looked straight into each other's eyes.

"I often think about nightmares that way. You've got to hold still. Don't run away. I understand that you may need to get up, walk around, and pour some water to get ahold of yourself. But don't leave what you just dreamed."

I introduced Robert to ways he could establish safety in himself: purposeful breathing; orienting to his environment to realize where he was; tracking his body sensations; comforting himself with a light touch on his chest or belly. "You've got to feel safe to do the work the nightmare is asking of you. And what is that? To step in and find a solution for the dilemma you're in when the dream ends."

So I imagine glass between me and the dream?

"You could, of course, but the glass is anything that helps you realize that you're not inside the glass with the gorilla; that is, that you're now out of the nightmare and nothing can harm you. All those safety practices I gave you, the breathing and so on, will keep you reminded that you're now safe."

Our time was coming to an end. I felt an urgency in Robert's voice when he asked,

"So, what comes next? Do I just stay there, right at the edge?"

"Write everything down in detail that you remember from the dream. Take the time to notice what feelings come up as you describe the details of the dream. The point is to get as close to your feelings as you can without being overwhelmed by them. If you need to pause, go outside, get fresh air. Splash water on your face if necessary. If it becomes too much, take a break—this shouldn't be thought of as failure. Be easy on yourself. But as much as you're able, describe in writing what you're feeling. Doing so will give you an outside point of view, which can help you feel more in control. Don't be surprised if you feel anger, or shame, or even anxiety that makes your body tremble. More than you realize now, allowing for feeling and recording these reactions is going to have a helpful effect on your nightmares, and especially your ability to stand your ground in the face of anything intimidating. You've already faced the nightmare with me, so it should be easier the second time through."

Robert turned away, contemplating all that I said. Then after a long pause, he made eye contact again.

"But ultimately, when you're ready, you go back into the dream, right where it ended. Step in carefully and slowly. Give your creative instincts a chance to read the situation, to see what's needed so that you can find a solution to the dilemma that the dream-you is caught in."

Robert looked at me questioningly.

"I have no idea what you'll do when you re-enter your dream and let it play forward. But study the scene. What does this man need? Not the bandaging. What does his soul need to come out of his shock? Then you wait. Linger in that moment, the one you usually wake out of. See what comes to mind. It will come as an impulse, some unexpected word or action.

When it does, try it out and see if it feels like an honest thing to do or say in your imagination."

I wasn't sure that I would see Robert again. He made no gesture of appreciation upon leaving, not even a handshake. I felt his tentativeness and knew that it was best not to crowd him. He left without mentioning another appointment. But a couple of weeks later, Robert called. When I saw him again, he opened up right away.

> To be honest, when I left here, I never intended to return. Not that I disagreed with anything you said, but...

He hesitated. "It's a lot to take in," I said.

> Well, I've been at my limit. I couldn't imagine doing anything that would make me feel worse. But I couldn't get the idea out of my mind; that there was something I could do about the dream, the scene I'd been stuck in all this time.

> So, I was up one night. I'd had another war dream, and I thought of the zoo story—it was about 3 am. I decided to sit still, letting the nightmare be right there across the kitchen table from me, exactly as I remembered it. I was nervous as hell. "OK, for five minutes. I'll give it that." I planted myself. Did the breathing, as you said. I couldn't write yet, and nothing happened really, except—and this was a big except—I realized that if I stayed still, the urge to run gradually lessened. This was news to me.

> Eventually, I wrote it down, and I felt calmer and went back to bed.

> The next day I started going back to the dream, turning it over in my head, letting myself be there right at the edge. But I never stepped in. Never felt right. Besides, I have no idea what I would do.

"Why don't we go there now? You and me."

I had Robert circle back and forth between what he remembered from the dream and what he was feeling in his body, all the while reminding him as needed to maintain his full, slow breathing. In this way, he calmed his alarm and made room for a creative response to occur. Eventually, I posed a question.

"What's he going through, you-the-soldier in the dream?"

He doesn't want to wake out of it.

"Why is that?"

Robert hesitated; taking a deep long breath and let out a big sigh. "Can you let him tell you why he doesn't want to leave the numbness?"

It'll fuckin' hurt too much!

The pain?

No...

"Find your breath again, Robert." He steadied himself.

He doesn't want to face what he's got to come home to.

"And what is that?"

Robert's face flushes as he admits the inadmissible.

Isn't it obvious? I'm only half the man I was.

It is here that Robert tells the backstory of the dream. His early life was spent in Puerto Rico, where he was free to roam beaches and play unending games with his friends. This all changed when his parents divorced at age twelve. Robert lost contact with his father and moved with his mother to a small town in East Texas, where he disappeared into anonymity. He had suddenly become an outsider: a stranger with an accent when he dared to speak, and he only knew a few words of English at that. It was a painful disruption to the life he had known.

Robert eventually found his way. The rough and tumble sports of his childhood made him quick and instinctive, plus he was driven to excel, and as his body matured, he became strong and fearless, catapulting him to all-star status in high school. For this reason, sports were more than play. It was the arena in which he made himself into someone proud. With his newly won confidence, Robert found his sweetheart and married at graduation. But while his physical acuity was superb, he lagged academically and subsequently only found minimum-wage work after high school.

Robert joined the military to secure a better future, but after only a few months, his injury aborted his plans.

"Your life ended once before, Robert, when you were twelve. And like now, you were stripped of everything that gave you a feeling of belonging, of mattering."

> Yeah, but I had hope then. There was somebody I could be—I had a future.

"And now you can't be anybody because of your injury. Yes, the loss has stolen everything you once used to make a new life when you came to this country. But let me ask, how did you get from the twelve-year-old who was bullied to be the star of your team? Did you do it alone?

> Of course not.

"Who was there for you?"

Robert gave a long and thoughtful pause, maybe studying the question for the first time.

> In the beginning, only my mom. Then there was a coach who noticed me, Coach Baber.

Robert's voice distinctly softened as he spoke of the man.

> He kept coming by the house to encourage me. He knew I was shy; I didn't know the language.

"He saw something in you."

> Yep, he took me under. He stopped the bullying and gave me a reason to come to school.

"What memory stands out the most about him?"

Robert sat up strong in his chair and took a big breath, preparing himself.

He had come around sports practice when I was in middle school to scout out potential players. After that, he would sometimes stop by the house on his way home to pay my mom and me a visit. Whenever I would come to the door, he would always shake my hand and call me by my last name: "Mr. Burgos," he would say.

Robert paused. His face flushed again, emotion rising to the surface.

He always looked me straight in the eyes when he spoke to me that way as if I were already a man, respected. It was the first time anyone had ever offered me a handshake.

"Really? What was the handshake like?"
Robert pause again, taking a deep breath to settle himself.

His hand was huge, compared to mine, and he shook my hand firmly but gently, not trying to overpower me. He kept holding my hand for a few seconds while he looked into my eyes. I wanted to turn away, 'cause it was so uncomfortable at first until I learned to accept his respect.

"So, he pulled you through those early years."
Robert turned away, obviously affected, as if studying something outside the window. While still looking away, he described an incident when the coach dropped in on middle school football practice.

At the end of practice one day, we were gathered on the field to hear Coach Baber talk about what lay ahead for us in high school, "if you play with all your hearts," he said. I still remember that phrase. He used it a lot. We all looked up to him because he was a local legend in our little town. He had taken the high school team to state many times.

Just when his pitch was about over, he looked over to me, kneeling in the back of the crowd. "Now I hear there's someone new in town, from somewhere else: Mr. Burgos." He paused while everyone looked around to see who that was. No one knew me by my full name. "He could be your leader one day," he said. Then he gave a warning. "Best you treat him well, or I may have to call on you."

I was shocked. Everybody got quiet. I wanted to hide, but I couldn't.
I felt myself grow big.

"And that ended the bullying?" Robert nodded yes, his eyes now softened, no longer stoic.

"How about we go back into the dream now?" Robert turned back into the room and closed his eyes.

"Your man in the dream has no one on his side, except for your wife who, as you say, is getting weary. If I were that man, and I felt I had no one to come home to—I mean someone who would do for me what Coach Baber did—I wouldn't want to wake up either."

Silence. Eyes still closed.

"It's up to you now, Robert. You've got to do the impossible, just like Coach did for you. You've got to get the one stuck in the dream to believe in himself. How will you do that? Take all the time you need."

Robert's breathing calmed. He seemed to have finally relaxed with the mention of his mentor's name. Robert took a long time in the silence, which lasted a couple of minutes, so long that I wondered if he had checked out and gotten lost in fantasy. Then I saw the slightest movement in his right hand. Gradually he began to open it, slowly, while sliding it down the top of his right leg as if reaching for something.

"Yeah, that's right. Reach in and get hold of him, Robert." That's when he closed his right hand firmly. A few moments later he lifted his left hand to his face, slowly placing his thumb and index finger over his eyes as he squeezed them tighter, but he could not stop the tears.

I've seen this happen a few times in my life, especially with men. Grief comes up and wants to be expressed, yet the man fears the vulnerability and tries to hold it back. A convulsion-like shaking took over Robert's entire body. He would not let himself cry, at least not openly, and in attempting to push back his tears, his body shook from the buildup of inner pressure. Robert's body bounced up and down on the chair, spasming from a war going on inside himself. All the while he covered his face with his hands.

After a very long minute, Robert settled and opened his eyes. He appeared relieved, but he looked at me questioningly, disoriented by the upheaval of strong, bodily emotion. I nodded my head approvingly.

"Good," I said, "you've made contact. I'm proud. Now, what do you do with him, this part of you that got left behind in the war? He needs your guidance."

Robert had no plans. He had essentially dropped out of life after losing his leg.

"What do you do for work, Robert?"

Nothing that matters.

I asked why he had not learned a trade or gone to college.

I've never been good in school

"Was that true in Puerto Rico?"

No, not at all, but here I've always been behind.

"You had a lot to catch up on, and not knowing the language put you at a big disadvantage. I bet you that you formed an idea about yourself, that you weren't smart in academics; that sports were the only way to achieve success. But is that true?

Silence.

"Tutors can be coaches, too, and bring you up to speed when you're behind. If you become a team player again and get other people around you, just like in sports, you can accomplish what you could never do alone."

During the remainder of our meeting, we discussed what a new life might look like: Education, a job and career he would love, a family.

As Robert was leaving, I handed him the name of a vet who ran a group for wounded warriors. He took the name, and for the first time, he shook my hand.

A couple of months later, I spoke with the leader of the veteran's group and learned that Robert had become a regular member. Like many men I have known, once Robert discovered he had a safe place to reveal his worst fears and biggest challenges, he formed deep bonds with other men. Not long afterward, he entered the local community college. When I heard this, I knew that there would be no stopping him.

The Witch
I Finally Faced

Writing about my dream of almost being eaten by a witch when I was a boy is a tricky undertaking. Without intending to, I could perpetuate a stereotype that has contributed to the deaths of millions of innocent people, mostly women, since ancient times to the present.

As you will read, and as I came to understand many years later, my childhood dream of being pursued by a hungry witch was a fitting symbol of a psychological danger I faced as a child, but it was one that I found impossible to admit. The feminine can not only give and sustain life, but as my dream intended to show, when harmed and out of balance, it can also take and even exploit. This dual capacity of the feminine runs counter to the tendency to idealize women and especially mothers, who are thought and wished to be all good, even when they are not.

Tragically, in much of the world, this symbolic nature of the witch has not been understood. Viewed literally, she has been feared and hated as the epitome of evil. But in truth, she is the creation of a highly superstitious mind, very often male, that believes there are powerful unseen and dangerous forces external to us. With unquestioned hostility, others are identified as collaborators (usually women) with these dark threatening powers. By persecuting and killing them off, the world might be safer. Thus, the mass hysteria of witch trials that swept through Europe for three centuries.

There are, of course, laudable qualities and powers of the so-called witch, most notably magic, the ability to transcend the limits of rational thought and access unusual creativity. She is the guardian of the medicinal secrets of Nature. And in contrast to our commercialization of youth, aging is not abhorrent to her. Additionally, unlike the naive and submissive female wished for by the authoritarian, hyper-masculine mind, the witch embodies cleverness and deep autonomy.

I will not address these and other aspects of the witch because she was none of these things for me. Instead, when I dreamed of her as a boy, she was a frightening figure that wanted to eat me. I have had to come to terms with this aspect of the witch. With this said, let me tell you about one of the most terrifying experiences of my life and how it became a source of unexpected wisdom.

I was five years old when she burst into my world. I had no preparation before her startling appearance. Her grasping fingers, long, bony, and gnarled, reached for me as heavy fat and age sagged from her outstretched arms.

Instinctively my body jolted to the right, attempting to flee her clutch. My panicked eyes, looking back, were glued on her warty face and opened hungry mouth, which showed a few long teeth and a ghastly crooked nose that hung above them, shaped more like an eagle's beak looking for its prey. Her larger-than-life ears were wide and long and could certainly out-hear my own.

My boy-feet were swift, quick to respond, but I was young and no match for her cunning and guile. As soon as I rushed from her, I became weak, my panicked legs quickly coming to a halt. Helplessly paralyzed, I awoke in terror.

This is my first remembered dream.

I have wondered more times than I can count, "Why would a young boy, without a means of protecting himself, be thrown into such a dire predicament? What did the dream have in mind, if indeed it was purposeful when it visited such terror on me?"

I have listened to dreams for a long time, and as is apparent in this book, I've taken a special interest in those dreams that disturb us, as if they have an importance beyond the others that can be more easily ignored. These difficult dreams are weighty, sharp-pointed, and intrusive, seeming to have been intentionally created so that we do not forget them.

I have also wondered about first dreams, the ones that come to us, sometimes, repeatedly, in our early years. Of all the dreams we had—and there were undoubtedly many, since children dream more than adults—why do we remember certain ones and not others?

Based on the childhood dreams told to me by adults, I have often suspected that the few dreams we do remember from childhood are filled with valuable information, pointing to the issues we must navigate and make sense of throughout our lives. This is certainly true for me, but it would take me decades before I understood the witch's intention in coming to me when I was a young boy.

I began to ponder my nightmare when I started seriously studying my dreams at midlife. As onerous as it was, I wondered if the dream contained a truth that could help me? Was there an intelligence orchestrating this dream? And if so, what did it have in mind when it fashioned this bewildering experience of being chased by a hungry witch?

In previous chapters, I mentioned the truth-telling function of dreams: they show us what we need to know but find difficult to accept. The truth may be threatening, unsettling, or may demand inconvenient changes to our lives. I have asked, "What might have been the sobering truth that the witch dream intended to show me?"

In reflecting on my life at the time of the dream, I would say that there was a predominant tone in my home: piousness. We earnestly strove to be morally righteous before a fundamentalist Christian God that expected us, his small remnant of true believers, to be faithful and exemplary of his commands and teachings. There could be no dancing since it would likely incite sexual desire, which was to be reserved for marriage. No card games of any kind could be played since this might lead to gambling. Neither was rock music allowed because of the possible inclusion of erotically suggestive lyrics. Most of all, we were to be obedient to God, parents, and country.

Despite daily Bible readings, prayer, and frequent church meetings every week, I came upon a foreboding presence in my house one day, which left me deeply disturbed. I discovered it around the time of the witch dream and before I had experienced violence within my home, which I discussed in previous chapters. On a beautiful summer afternoon, I walked from the living room onto the screened porch of our working-class apartment just outside Mobile, Alabama. Above me and in my periphery, I noticed movement. Looking upwards, I beheld a giant black spider creeping across the ceiling, its body crawling upside down. Perhaps startled as much as me, it scurried away and disappeared into a hole in the corner of the ceiling, which until that moment I had never known existed.

A chill came over me. I had assumed that I was safe in my house. An unaccustomed sensation took hold of me. It was my first remembered experience of dread. With it came an unsettling realization: my family and I were not alone. Something else lived with us, and it was stealthy, dark, and dangerous.

The great majority of events from childhood are not remembered. Thus, the ones that do survive are noteworthy. Knowing this, I have asked myself, "Why does the memory of the steely spider endure, and why do I recall it when I remember my nightmare of the witch?"

For many years, decades actually, I could not bear the truth of what some part of me perceived as a boy. There was treachery in my house. By all outer appearances, however, my home was safe and everyone within it well-intentioned. Yet, dreaming intelligence—from my perspective now as a studied adult—wanted me to know something contrary to all that I presumed. However, it would take five more decades before I could fully bear the sobering truth of the spider and the witch.

I was in my early fifties when I inhaled a compound used for centuries in the Amazonian rainforest to induce visions. A trusted psychologist colleague trained to work with therapeutic psychedelics sat beside me as I quickly entered another world. As the power of the visionary medicine took hold of me, I was pulled downward, and surrendering to it, I landed in a darkened space. With eyeshades on, I peered into the darkness, but no images came into view. However, after a few more seconds, I knew that I was in a strangely familiar place. I had returned to a foreboding forest thick with uncertainty and danger, and there was no doubt that I was not alone. A few seconds more, I realized I had re-entered my childhood imagination and was in one of the two fairy tales I had my parents read to me countless times.

Hansel and Gretel, along with Rapunzel, fascinated me. Though I did not realize it consciously, I instinctively knew that I shared their struggle. A witch had imprisoned these three unfortunate children. I now know that I had my parents read these stories repeatedly because I was searching for clues on how these hapless children had found their freedom. Now some fifty years later, I had landed back in the forest with Hansel and Gretel, and I sensed the witch's house nearby. The door was partially opened.

I knew that it was my task to walk into the darkened, eerie house and free Hansel from the cage where he was still being held while the witch fattened him up before she was to eat him.

I was not pretending or making this up. As those who have entered such visionary states know, the experience happens to you as if orchestrated by an intelligence other than your own. I was taken back into this mythic childhood scene quite unexpectedly, never intending to go there. A consciousness other than my willpower had directed me. I was not only surprised, but perplexed. I thus posed a crucial question, "What do you wish to show me?"

The answer came in no uncertain words: "Incest," it said. "You were incested."

These words were cruel and grievous to bear. I protested, "No! Not me. Not in my safe Christian home. And certainly not by my dear mother, whom I love and who without a doubt loves me." Yet, like a house of cards collapsing, there was no going back to my illusory idealism. Uttered as clearly as if spoken by my trusted journey guide, who sat quietly beside me, I could not deny the truth of what had been said.

I knew the reference to incest was emotional, not physical or explicitly sexual. Nevertheless, a boundary had been crossed, the results of which had been damaging to me and had denied me a fundamental birthright: to live freely and true to myself without having to surrender a part of me to satisfy another.

I entered the witch's house, and there she was, as large and imposing as she had been in my five-year-old dream. Only this time, I did not run.

Usually, intense visionary experiences are so immersive that all you can do is lay on your back, breathe consciously to steady awareness, and witness what you are given. However, I knew I was in for a struggle, and I thus felt a need to engage my strength and tenacity. I turned over onto my hands and knees and dug my fingers into the rug like claws into the earth. I braced myself and engaged the witch with the force of my will. I knew that I must take back what had been stolen. I willed back my power from her, and as I did, she became incrementally smaller. As the imposing witch shrank, my diminutive boy body grew larger, eventually leaving the once over-powering witch diminished and me fully grown.

In the days that followed, I knew that something profound had taken shape inside me, but it was not until a phone call the following week that I realized the effect of my mythic journey. When I answered, I could hear familiar anguish in my mother's voice. Once again, foregoing a customary "How are you?" greeting, she immediately launched into a tearful lamentation of how wretched it would be to spend eternity apart from me: she in heaven and me in hell. Even though I had left fundamentalism decades before, my earnest mother continued to be distraught.

I understood her dilemma. She was so committed to her religious belief that she believed anyone who did not expressly take (and keep) Christ as their Savior would languish eternally in the fires of hell. I suspected, too, that it wasn't so much her dread of me burning that concerned her in that phone call, as it was the separation that would befall us if I did not renounce my "secular ways and come back to Jesus."

My mother struggled with shame throughout her life, though I doubt that she ever named it as such. It was more likely that she felt herself to be ever in need of forgiveness. Her feeling of being tainted likely started early in her life under the harsh upbringing of her morally righteous father, for whom, in her eyes, and maybe his, she could never be good enough. I remember how often my mother would leave her parents' house, distraught, crying in the front seat of the car as we drove away, once again wounded by stinging criticisms from her father.

When my mother had a conversion experience in her mid-forties, she told me that she felt unconditional love for the first time in her life. I believe the experience was genuine and life-altering. However, the experience did not erase the conditioning of previous decades in which she was unworthy in her father's critical eyes. Consequently, my mother held to her newly found faith with pious austerity, still striving to be good enough, even twice in her life fasting for forty days on water alone to purify herself as Jesus had done. Unfortunately for me, she could not see that others might find their way to the divine in a different manner than what she had found.

Without knowing it, my mother had attempted to live her life through me. By making me her Golden boy pure, good and righteous, she could at least by proxy establish her own goodness and right standing before God. But the spiritual path I had taken had thwarted her plans. This became apparent one day when she made a painful discovery during a visit to me when I was in my late thirties.

Having only one bed at the time, I allowed my father and mother to sleep in my bedroom while I slept on my couch. Later, when I returned home at the end of the day from an outing with my girlfriend, I walked into a house full of angst and despair. My mother was weeping because she had inadvertently found contraceptives in a drawer beside my bed. Her idealism of me had suffered a crushing blow. Because of the church's strict moral code, she had always assumed I would remain a virgin until marriage. She never expected that her pious son would depart from the True Faith and commit fornication.

I felt incensed when I saw my mother's despondent state, though I held my feelings back in the face of her grief and despair. Years later, however, when I received the phone call just a few days after having taken my power and dignity back from the witch, something instinctual rose up in me and finally said, " No more!" Like a volcanic eruption, the protest came from the depths of me: "I will no longer take these intrusive phone calls, these judgments and presumptions that my faith is inferior to yours." Then, with the same strength of will that I had used to rescue my power from the witch, I demanded, "You must release me. You must allow God to be the judge of me. Who are we to sit in judgment of one another? Is this not God's prerogative?"

My mother was startled but not convinced. She continued pleading, urging me to return to the faith. It was then that I laid down the ultimate. "If you do not allow me my freedom to choose," I said with an authority that even surprised me, "I will never see you again. I will love you, but only from a distance. I feel disrespected by you when you treat me this way. You must stop. This has gone on long enough!"

Once off the phone with my mother, I called her minister, letting her know my firm intention. Given my mother's trust in her pastor, I thought she might have a way of speaking with my mother so that she could find it in her heart to relinquish her role as protector and director of my life. Indeed, that is what happened.

From that day forward, my mother never made a demand on me. She was the embodiment of sweetness, full of encouragement and appreciation for the son she had. She still did not agree with nor understand why I did yoga (an eastern form of false religion to her), nor did she have respect for psychology ("man's way of pulling himself up without the grace of God"), but she rested her case and let me, and herself, off the hook. Over the next five and final years of her life, my mother was a joy to be around.

At her funeral, the church was filled with affectionate friends who were grateful for my mother's reassuring presence. In fact, she was known paradoxically as "having the gift of encouragement." I knew that I had to say something. I could not ignore my painful history with my mother, for indeed, it had everything to do with what my mother had eventually accomplished.

"Everyone here knows," I said from behind the pulpit where family members could speak, "that Evelyn, my mother, was devout and deeply spiritual. This is no secret. She enjoyed your fellowship because you shared her heartfelt commitment to God. But near the end of my mother's life, she discovered something even more important than her faith." I paused and let this assertion hang in mid-air, causing all present to be alert for any dismissal of their religion.

I then read a passage from the Bible, "And now abide faith, hope, and love, these three; but the greatest of these is love (New International Version, 1978, I Cor. 13:13)." I added, "In the last five years of her life, my mother found what was greater than faith. It was during this time that she was able to transcend our differences and find her way to the greatest gift that she ever gave me: a mother's unconditional love."

Though the sanctuary was filled to overflowing, everyone fell silent. No one stirred or made a sound, for no one could be unaffected by my sincerity as I spoke with trembling voice and tears in my eyes. For a moment, it seemed to me that we were all on common ground.

It had taken me nearly fifty years to complete the nightmare that intruded on me at the tender age of five. It was a significant accomplishment to find my way through the fear and the shame that had been imposed on me by a desperate mother and an autocratic God. But eventually, I trusted the authority of my primal voice and said, "No."

A Return to the Question

I have turned a question over in my mind a thousand times throughout the years, "What was Nature doing when it dreamed that dreadful nightmare?" I have finally come to an answer. As torturous as it was, the dream showed me what no one would admit in the light of day.

As a boy, I adored my mother. My father offered financial stability as a steady blue-collar worker. He never complained about the load he carried, but it was my mother who provided emotional warmth. Another dynamic also allied me with my mother: she was highly distressed over the "failure of her marriage." I was much too young to be told this, but more than once, she warned me to "never make the mistake" that she had made "by marrying the wrong person."

Knowing my mother's distress and witnessing the many unresolved arguments between her and my father, I hoped to avoid my mother's demise by finding the perfect partner. A telling incident comes to mind that conveys the depth of the compelling romantic myth that overtook me in my attempt to avoid the suffering my mother endured. The memory comes from around the time of the witch dream.

I am kneeling at my bed and saying prayers with my mother beside me. Though I remember only this one night, the prayer I made was likely offered numerous times. Already feeling the weight of my mother's marital distress, I pleaded, "Please, God, begin preparing the right woman for me."

The poignant memory gives me empathy for the plight I faced. Salvation would come to me through the Lover, the Perfect Other. Yes, this led to painful breakups with good and more than adequate women who loved me. They could not fit into the mold cast by my romantic longing to find The One, and only one, prepared for me by the Divine. When I found her, I would certainly know because there would be no distress or disappointment like my mother faced with her down-to-earth, flesh-and-blood husband who brought her many disappointments.

Carl Jung believed that one function of dreams is to compensate or counterbalance extreme positions we adopt in waking life (Jung, 1968). You can see this compensatory function at work in my witch dream. Already at an early age, I was taken over by an idealization of my mother and of some yet-to-be woman who would assure me of a better life. The witch dream and the encounter with the dangerous spider lurking in the hidden regions of our house countered the extreme naivete of the romantic boy that I was, desperate to find a solution for the suffering that existed in our home.

Alice Miller (2001) has written about our plight as children with more empathy than most. She articulates an important insight: we can endure and survive a great deal of distress, even abuse, if we have at least one person, an "enlightened witness," who bears witness to the truth of what we suffer. If there is such an adult in our lives, be that a relative, friend, teacher, or mentor, who speaks empathetically to us and confirms the wrong being done, our dignity is protected. We are thus less likely to turn to extremes of violence, self-abuse, or addictions to console ourselves.[6]

Dreams often serve this truth-telling function. Indeed, for some, a remembered childhood dream may be the only truthful account of what was otherwise suffered in silence. I consider my early witch dream to be just that, a faithful witness that deftly gave me an experience of the true predicament in which I was caught.

If I were to put the message of the witch dream into words, it would be this:

> All is not well. You're not always safe, neither in your home nor
> even in the presence of the feminine, which you expect to nurture
> and protect you. Lest you be caught unaware, beware.

Of course, I could not have grasped these things cognitively as a five-year-old boy, but there are other ways of knowing, especially through direct experience, which dreams are. Now, as an adult man and someone who has suffered the loss of that early idealism that once protected me from hopelessness and yet made me vulnerable, I would add to the early warning I received through the dream.

> A parent can harm you as well as love you. Someone who cherishes
> you may also diminish you. It's up to you to stay aware and know
> what's true so that you are protected and do not naively fall prey
> to ill-treatment either maliciously or unknowingly done to you.

---

6. See Miller's astute review of Hitler's childhood in For Your Own Good (1983) and the consequences that ensued as a result of him lacking a compassionate witness of the insidious abuses he suffered under his totalitarian father.

The Witch Within

To add to the richness of my dream, I will recount another encounter with the witch a few years after my visionary experience of freeing Hansel. This confrontation showed me first-hand how abusive forces can get embedded in us and pull us into becoming them.

I set out on a beautiful trail in the Virginia mountains, where I then lived, hoping to find my way out of my despair over the loss of a romantic relationship. A woman I had put my hopes on lost interest in me, and I suffered greatly. Bewildered and tormented by the loss, I knew that I was in trouble, but I did not know what to do with the desperation and hunger to remain in contact with her. Pondering my predicament, I rounded a bend on the canopy trail, which hung on the side of a mountain just above a steep ravine, and I suddenly felt afraid. It was not the height that made me dizzy. I had come upon a dangerous presence.

Looking around, I saw nothing alarming, so I tried pushing my anxiety aside and moving ahead, but I could not. My feet were fixed to the ground. Therefore, I turned to the apprehension I felt and asked, "What is the danger you are alerting me to?"

The answer caused me to become unsteady: the hungry witch was nearby, just around the bend in the trail. Though my eyes could not see her, her presence was as real as she had been the day I encountered her in the dark forest of Hansel and Gretel. I felt her voracious appetite waiting for me. I then suffered a humbling truth: I had become the witch, empty and obsessed.

That day I looked into the mouth of my own narcissism, concerned only with what I wanted, attempting to fill my void by forcing love on another. The sobering vision broke the obsession that had a hold on me. I then realized that being self-absorbed and imposing an agenda on someone else can be a changing role. We all are susceptible to such strong currents in our personalities.

Seeing the witch as a capacity within me confronted me with a task: "You must feed her," a wise voice said from inside me. I knew what this meant. I could pathologize myself and attribute my romantic compulsion to co-dependency and other pejorative diagnoses, but eventually, I had to find a way to acknowledge the painful emptiness I carried and bring understanding and compassion to it.

As I stood in the middle of the mountain trail, contemplating the challenge, a memory came. I was about five years old, and two friends had come to visit me for the afternoon, brother and sister, Bubba and Wanda Lee. As an only child the first eight years of my life, I relished their company, so much that when dusk settled, and they announced that it was time for them to return home, I protested. I remembered that I could not bear the anticipated loneliness, and I closed the door to my bedroom where we had been playing and stood guard so that they could not pass. Of course, they resisted, and I was no match for their combined strength. So, I resorted to the last deterrent that might keep them with me. Quickly grasping each of their arms one after the other, I bit into their flesh. While this did not deter them, it did send them home with teeth marks welling up on tender, innocent skin. It was not long afterward that my mother received a call from their mother, and I was sorely reprimanded.

This memory had always been a source of embarrassment for me. However, as I encountered the hungry witch as myself on the forest trail, I became compassionate for the boy that indeed was empty and afraid of that emptiness, the one who had no one to explain how to cope with the loneliness that threatened to overwhelm him.

Sometimes it is enough to show compassion for the suffering we once endured. Still standing on the trail, I finally intervened after many years, returning to that early memory with empathy for the frightened boy who was desperate to keep his friends with him. In the middle of the forest, I knelt beside young Len, who was alone and bewildered after his friends had rushed out the door, and I named the painful loneliness that no one had ever described. I showed him compassion for the very first time. Having seen him and not judged him, we both felt great relief, and I thus completed an unfinished memory that had started decades before.

The journey with the witch has been long, winding, and at times treacherous. Initially, as a boy, I was in danger of being eaten by her. The dream warned me and awakened some part of me to the peril I faced. Decades later, the witch re-appeared (in my visionary experience), and I found the power to resist her and take back what had been stolen. Afterward, in what became my most intimate encounter with her, I was humbled to discover the witch as a capacity within me, just as capable of doing harm as had been done to me.

Now her terrible mask has fallen. Her voracious appetite that I long feared, which also became mine, is no longer repugnant to me. I visit with her daily and feed her as best I can. I do this by listening respectfully to what the hunger inside me needs. I often find that my yearning can be fulfilled by simply pausing and focusing on beauty in any of its myriad expressions around me. But more than anything, it is empathy that fills the emptiness, compassion for the longing simply to be loved and understood for who we are.

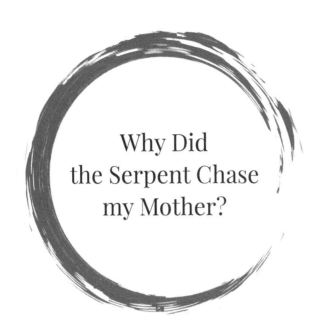

Why Did
the Serpent Chase
my Mother?

I have spent a good amount of time thinking about this question, especially after becoming a psychologist and working with my own dreams, some of which involved snakes. Assuming that you have read the story of my mother's nightmares in chapter one and how I was frightfully awakened by them, you will perhaps understand why answering this question has taken on such significance for me. Why would a woman who was earnestly devoted to her faith and family be persecuted in her dreams throughout her life by the aggressive appearance of a snake that she considered sinister? There is, of course, another question that goes hand in hand with this one: Why did my mother run from the snake, in fact, well into her eighties, even into the last few months of her life?

To most, the answer to this latter question would seem obvious. After all, it was a *snake*, and most humans have a cautionary, if not phobic, response to them. Not everyone, however, runs from them in their dreams, and certainly not all snakes chase a dreamer. This dual presence of chasing and running in my mother's dreams indicates an unusually intense conflict. As a dream worker, this tells me that a lot is at stake. Something highly charged is happening, but what might that be?

You might very well ask another question: Why should you be concerned or even interested in investigating the above questions? After all, this is my mother I am talking about, so why would her story be beneficial to you?

I believe that my mother's fear of the snake in her dreams is not her story alone but reflects a dilemma most of us face in our culture. How we care for, deny, or indulge our instinctual, earthen (serpentine) nature has everything to do with whether we know the satisfying fulfillment of wholeness or the anguish of fragmentation.

To explain this more fully, I will review two ancient and quite divergent views about serpent power that, unbeknownst to most, affect us every day. These two world views have much to do with how we think about and respond to nightmares in general, not only those involving snakes but anything that threatens us in dreams.

The Enduring Ancient Influences of the Power of the Serpent

Though not realized by most, our culture is influenced by two opposing ideas about the power symbolized by the serpent. The most popular view—that the snake represents sexual desire—comes from both Freud (who has been criticized for reducing dream figures to cloaked symbols of sexual desire) and several centuries of Christian theology and art. In traditional Christianity, the serpent is the personification of evil and temptation and has its origin in the Biblical Garden of Eden creation account. Here we see that Adam and Eve were created and lived in an idyllic paradise, which they could enjoy as long as they did not disobey and succumb to temptation. In the middle of their lavish garden, God placed two trees and warned Adam and Eve never to eat the fruit of "the tree of the knowledge of good and evil," since it would destroy their innocence, nor should they eat from "the tree of immortality," because it would enable them to live eternally like God.

Many centuries of the Christian rendering of this story has reduced Eve's temptation to that of sexual desire—the apple becoming the colloquial image for this. Out of curiosity, Eve supposedly succumbed to the snake's seduction and ate the forbidden fruit from the tree of the knowledge of good and evil. For this reason, she was banished, along with Adam, from their idyllic life, having become conscious and ashamed of their nakedness. But given the gravity of this one sin, the expulsion from paradise was not enough. To add to Eve's punishment, she and all women after her would suffer two more ordeals: pain in childbirth and domination by their husbands.

> To the woman God said, "I will make your pains in childbearing very severe; with painful labor you will give birth to children. And your desire will be for your husband, and he will rule over you. (New International Version, 1978, Gen. 3:16).

Adam was also punished, and all men who came after him:

> To Adam, he said, "Because you listened to your wife and ate fruit from the tree about which I commanded you, 'You must not eat from it,' "Cursed is the ground because of you; through painful toil you will eat food from it all the days of your life. It will produce thorns and thistles for you, and you will eat the plants of the field. By the sweat of your brow, you will eat your food until you return to the ground since from it you were taken; for dust you are and to dust you will return. (New International Version, 1978, Gen. 3:16).

The serpent received punishment as well:

> So the Lord God said to the serpent, "Because you have done this, Cursed are you above all livestock and all wild animals! You will crawl on your belly, and you will eat dust all the days of your life.

And I will put enmity between you and the woman, and between your offspring and hers; he will crush your head, and you will strike his heel." (New International Version, 1978, Gen. 3:16)

Julius Schnorr von Carolsfeld, 1852-60

The Garden of Eden story, the most ubiquitous creation myth in western civilization that has endured into our time, informed, without question, my Bible-believing mother's response to the snake that chased her. The Genesis account was referred to often in our church, and it certainly taught my mother to fear and despise the snake. It had seduced our innocent parents and was ultimately responsible for humanity's expulsion from paradise. My mother took the story literally and without question. But therein was the problem.

What my mother did not know, and she is not alone in this, is that "our" creation myth—for indeed it is the most prominent one that endures in western civilization—was written not only for theology but for politics as well. This was shocking for me to discover. When I read *The Mythology of Eden* by Arthur and Elena George (2014), I learned that the biblical creation story was written at a crucial time in Hebrew and world history. Before the emergence of patriarchal sky gods that came to rule the cosmos, religious symbols of the divine were primarily feminine in form. After all, early humans saw that females gave birth, and because of this, the divine was naturally conceived of as feminine.

Gradually masculine deities emerged, sharing the divine council of gods with female deities. By the time the Genesis account was written, earth-based religions, based on reverence for agriculture and the seasons, were populated by both male and female deities. However, severe forms of patriarchy expanded and began pushing these ancient cultures aside. To accomplish this, those advocating for a singular masculine sky god needed to provide a religious justification for establishing dominance.

Most people, like myself, have associated Judaism, from which Christianity emerged, with monotheism (the belief that there exists only one true God) and that this divinity is masculine (God the *Father*). But Judaism has not always been so. In fact, for hundreds of years Yahweh, the god of ancient Israel, was only one of several gods who shared divinity with other gods, and at least one of these revered divinities was female. Asherah, who was worshipped under sacred trees and by other tokens of nature, came to be hated and despised by a minority of radical patriarchal conservatives who wished to stamp out any form of earth-based goddess worship among the Hebrews. Much of what Christians call the Old Testament is filled with diatribes against those who worshipped "false gods," which often involved symbols of Asherah, "the queen of heaven."

> You shall not plant for yourself an Asherah of any kind of tree beside the altar of the Lord your God, which you shall make for yourself. (New International Version, 1978, Deut. 16:21)

The populace often pushed back whenever the hyper-Yahweh-exclusivists sought to eradicate people's love for and loyalty to the divine feminine.

> ...we will certainly carry out every word that has proceeded from our mouths, by burning sacrifices to the queen of heaven and pouring out drink offerings to her, just as we ourselves, our forefathers, our kings, and our princes did in the cities of Judah and in the streets of Jerusalem; for then we had plenty of food and were well off and saw no misfortune. But since we stopped

burning sacrifices to the queen of heaven and pouring out drink offerings to her, we have lacked everything and have met our end by the sword and by famine. (New International Version, 1978, Jer. 44:17-19)

The Genesis creation story not only relates how things came to be, but it was written to dethrone the goddess, as represented by Eve, and humiliate the serpent, a primary symbol of the sacred life force in religions of the ancient world. The Genesis account of creation and the fall (of humans) provides a religious justification for the extreme patriarchal and radical exclusivists (Yahweh only) who sought to dominate women and link our earthen impulses, like sexuality and deep autonomy, with evil. By *deep autonomy*, I refer to following one's internal sense of right and wrong vs. acquiescing in obedience to an autocratic god outside of (and sometimes contrary to) one's own nature.

I, of course, never knew any of what I have just summarized about the intention of the author(s) of the creation story. Nor did my mother. But despite being an earnest Christian boy, there was something about the Garden of Eden story that troubled me, though it took me many years before I could articulate it. The Genesis creator god is intolerant and punitive. After only one infraction of the law (eating the fruit from the tree of the knowledge of good and evil), Adam and Eve were expelled from paradise, along with all humanity after them, and were made to suffer thereafter through painful childbirth and domination, if female, and distressful physical labor, if male. Furthermore, as if to stack the deck against Adam and Eve, the temptation that they succumbed to had been placed right in front of them, in the unavoidable center of paradise by God himself. Even as a child, this felt cruel to me. I wondered and secretly complained, "What kind of parent would intentionally tempt their children and then harshly punish them for losing self-control?"

As described in the scriptures following the creation account, this same god later sanctioned mass genocide of the inhabitants of Palestine ("the land of Canaan"), which God's chosen people were commanded to invade and clear of false gods and all those worshipping them. Any honest and unbiased reading of the Biblical account will be disturbingly reminiscent of modern atrocities we read about today by radical Islamists who are "purging the infidels" from countries in the middle east and beyond.

> However, in the cities of the nations the Lord your God is giving you as an inheritance, do not leave alive *anything that breathes*. Completely destroy them—the Hittites, Amorites, Canaanites, Perizzites, Hivites, and Jebusites—as the Lord your God has commanded you. Otherwise, they will teach you to follow all the detestable things they do in worshiping their gods, and you will sin against the Lord your God. (New International Version, 1978, Deut. 20:16-18)

But even if you were part of God's special people, you were not safe if female. By law, if a woman gave no proof of virginity (by bleeding) on her wedding night, she was to be stoned to death at the door of her father's house. Additionally, disobedient children could likewise suffer the same punishment. Yes, these things are in the Bible.

> If a man takes a wife and, after sleeping with her, dislikes her... saying, "I married this woman, but when I approached her, I did not find proof of her virginity.... If...the charge is true and no proof of the young woman's virginity can be found, she shall be brought to the door of her father's house and there the men of her town shall stone her to death. She has done an outrageous thing in Israel by being promiscuous while still in her father's house. You must purge the evil from among you. (New International Version, 1978, Deut. 22:13-2)

> If someone has a stubborn and rebellious son who does not obey his father and mother and will not listen to them when they discipline him, his father and mother shall take hold of him and bring him to the elders at the gate of his town. They shall say to the elders, "This son of ours is stubborn and rebellious. He will not obey us. He is a glutton and a drunkard." Then all the men of his town are to stone him to death. You must purge the evil from among

you. All Israel will hear of it and be afraid. (New International
Version, 1978, Deut. 21:18-21)

Admittedly, the Hebrew and Christian conception of God has evolved
and tempered itself over time, yet the creation story with the intolerant,
autocratic god has been read unquestioningly for centuries to the devout
and continues to be preached and lectured on without objection in syna-
gogues and churches the world over.

Alice Miller, author of For Your Own Good (1983), helped me understand
how such a cruel creation story could be written and accepted for several
millennia. Miller, a psychotherapist, writer, and astute observer of how
trauma is passed from one generation to another, says it is understandable
how such a story was crafted. It was, she says, written by men who had
endured similar harsh mistreatment by their own fathers when they were
children. Otherwise, how else could humans conceive of a merciless, unforgiving god if they had not experienced such vengefulness throughout
their childhood?

My mother's father, whose abusive behavior I described in the chapter,
Realizing Undermining Influences, certainly predisposed her to think of God
the Father as intolerant and unforgiving. Undoubtedly determining that
it was safer to acquiesce and attempt to win her father's favor rather than
protest his sternness, my mother tried in vain to earn his acceptance until
the end of his life. In the process, she learned never to challenge authority.
Thus, unquestioned obedience became a religious precept for my mother.
I even remember her reprimanding me more than once as a boy, saying,
"If I say white is black, and black is white, you believe it. Why?" And then
she would pause, waiting for an answer that I could never give, before
completing the lesson for me: "Because I am your parent!" From early on,
my mother, being first-born, had learned to adapt to merciless authority
to spare her from the overpowering force of her father, so therefore, why
shouldn't her Father in Heaven wield the same autocratic authority that
she had learned from her earthly one?

After being raised in a home and church that highly valued obedience,
it took me decades before I could let go of the belief that these ancient
men who inscribed their code of ethics into scripture knew better than I.

I can tell you that such an idea ultimately leads to a deep distrust of your own nature.

The snake is the counterpoint to unquestioned obedience. It is the epitome of that which resists control. Reptiles cannot be tamed because they lack the limbic system of the brain that makes emotions possible. Without this, they do not bond with or become submissive to humans like mammals. Snakes live pristinely true to themselves. They do what is needed to survive, not out of selfishness, but simply because their instincts cannot be undermined or manipulated. And in this sense, *the snake is the ultimate symbol of defiance to an autocratic god that insists on blind obedience.*

Remember that it was the serpent that questioned God in the Garden of Eden story.

> The woman said to the serpent, 'We may eat fruit from the trees in the garden, but God did say, "You must not eat fruit from the tree that is in the middle of the garden, and you must not touch it, or you will die."' 'You will not surely die,' the serpent said to the woman. 'For God knows that when you eat of it, your eyes will be opened, and you will be like God, knowing good and evil. (New International Version, 1978, Gen. 3: 2-4)

Indeed, what the serpent said was true. Adam and Eve's eyes *were* opened as the result of eating the fruit, and they became aware of the distinction between good and evil.

> When the woman saw that the fruit of the tree was good for food and pleasing to the eye, and also *desirable for gaining wisdom*, she took some and ate it. She also gave some to her husband, who was with her, and he ate it. Then the eyes of both of them were opened, and they realized that they were naked, so they sewed fig leaves together and made coverings for themselves. (New International Version, 1978, Gen. 3: 6-7)

Contrary to what many believe, the serpent did not deceive Eve, in the sense of lying to her. What it said was true. And its words appealed to her because she desired to grow in wisdom rather than maintain an idyllic life based on naivete and obedience. The serpent's so-called *wrongdoing* was that it caused Eve to question authority.

The Goodness of Our Earthen Nature

There is an alternative understanding of serpent imagery that also goes back into ancient times and remains with us still, but this perspective is quite positive regarding the serpent's power. Surprisingly, we come into contact with this other perspective every day. This alternate view sees the serpent, not as tempting us away from the divine, but as a symbol for the *essence* of the divine, the precious life force, which, if aligned with, will convey healing and vitality. The symbol for the serpent as Sacred Life Force can be seen in pharmacies, on ambulances, and in hospitals and doctor's offices every day. It is the caduceus.

Few people know that our symbol for healing in western medicine has its origin in temples that utilized dreams for diagnosis and treatment. Known throughout the ancient Grecian world as Asklepian Dream Heal-

ing Temples (Tick, 2001), they were complexes where mind-body medicine was at its zenith. The sick and diseased traveled great distances to take warm healing baths (something unusual in the ancient world), receive therapeutic massages, exercise in a special gymnasium, and participate in cathartic theatre before entering a room where they would sleep in search of a healing dream. Nonpoisonous snakes were purposely placed in the dream sanctuaries, and the most enduring symbol for these temples where people received healing dreams is the physician who attained sacred status, Asclepius, known for his staff that was encircled by a snake.

The Hippocratic Oath that some physicians still take to this day contains a reference to this father of dream healing medicine.

> I swear by Apollo the Physician and Asclepius, and Hygeia and Panacea (daughters of Asclepius) and all the gods and goddesses as my witnesses, that, according to my ability and judgment, I will keep this Oath and this contract (North, 2002).

You will find similar references to the serpent as a symbol of the sacred life force in ancient India. If you study yoga, especially the internal, meditative form, you will soon learn of a serpent that is curled at the base of the spine, representing dormant lifeforce that can be channeled upwards to the brain and beyond through the crown chakra. Known as Kundalini, it is represented as two snakes spiraling up the energy centers/nerve complexes of the body.

An Experimentation with Serpent Power

With this alternate life-giving view of the serpent, I borrowed a small python from a local pet store once and brought it to a weekend retreat I offered for several people studying with me. One of the members was a physician who had recently been diagnosed with terminal cancer. A few weeks before our retreat, he had dreamed of a snake and had attempted to kill it by stabbing it repeatedly with a knife.

When I heard the dream, I was not sure if the man's snake was symbolic of the deep internal life force that had come to help him, which he nevertheless feared. Or was it, as the doctor presumed, a sign of cancer spreading in his body?

Before the retreat, I kept the python in an aquarium in my home for a couple of days. Wanting to get acquainted with this curious creature, I took it out and holding it in front of me, I looked into its eyes. Immediately the words rang out loud in me, "The essence of evil."

I was chilled to the bones as I peered into an intelligence that was more primal than the life I lived. It scared me, and I wondered, "What is so threatening about this non-poisonous creature from a pet store?"

I could not name it then, and I now think that this was because I was still living contrary to the snake's nature. Without realizing it, I did not trust my deep autonomy. I questioned myself often. But not being conscious of this, I thus projected that which was forbidden onto the snake. When I looked into its eyes, it was not simply an animal, a reptile similar to a lizard. I saw my own unlived nature that had not been allowed to thrive in my formative years. Nor was I fully allowing it yet. In fact, it took a few more years before I could see that it was a deeper part of me that frightened me that day. It was precocious, astute, without gullibility or naivete, and lived true to itself.

As I put the snake back into the aquarium, a memory came to mind. A couple of years before, I had sat in a candlelit room with twenty people as a Peruvian shaman chanted and sang devotional songs to support us as we surrendered to the effects of the visionary tea ayahuasca. This was not my first time, but I found myself disturbingly anxious, anticipating danger as the sedative effects gently but assuredly pulled me downwards, attempting to take me to another dimension. In the twilight darkness of the room, I suddenly imagined that a snake was there, stealthy moving, eluding my eyesight, but all the while stalking me.

As a result of having done a good amount of dreamwork as well as visionary medicine work, I knew to turn and face the intimidating creature. I thus posed a question, "What do you want?" As if the snake was communicating, I became aware of the anger, actually bitterness, that I carried towards someone who had betrayed me. With the help of the visionary tea, I could then see myself in the future, several decades ahead. I was shocked to realize what had become of me. My vengeful anger had turned me into a shriveled up, sour old man.

The vision shocked me, and it proved to be the humbling element needed to get me out of my resentfulness and move me beyond the harm that had happened to me. This incident caused me to realize that it is not only the snake's capacity to sliver away and hide that frightens us. It correspondingly has the ability to find its way to our hiding places. The serpent is the part of us that cannot be deceived.

This memory lingered with me as I brought the python to the retreat a few days later. When we convened, I placed the snake in the middle of the floor, where we sat in a circle. Immediately, the snake started making its way around to each of us as we sat cross-legged, passing by and inspecting every group member. With one man who had once spoken to us about his "impotence," the snake crawled under his legs and emerged from his lap near his crotch. I am not fabricating this.

After this mesmerizing encounter, I put the snake away, and the group spread out over the yoga studio where we were gathered. The participants blindfolded themselves, lay down, and utilized a form of rapid breathing (Holotropic Breathwork) to enter a visionary state (like wakeful dreaming) as I played evocative music. After about an hour, I turned the music off and brought the experience to a close. Everyone took their eye masks off and began to come back into a circle, except the physician, who remained blindfolded. He began moving about the room slowly on hands and knees. We all respectfully watched since it appeared that he was still in an exploratory state. I felt an intuition to bring the snake out again.

Moving slowly and quietly, I placed the snake on the back of the man's hands which were turned palms down to the floor. I then walked away to observe. Although still blindfolded, the physician immediately recognized the snake and tenderly picked it up in his hands. As he cradled the snake's body close to his bosom, he let out a grievous moan and then expressed a moving apology: "Please forgive me," he pleaded, weeping, "I did not know what I was doing." It was a riveting moment. It appeared to us that he was referring to his murderous aggression towards the snake of his dream but not only that. I also had the impression that he was expressing grief over having lived many years neglecting if not abusing a precious part of himself.

Shortly after the retreat, even with a terminal diagnosis, the doctor moved out on his own and spent several weeks living alone. "It's essential that I do this," he explained. I did not learn the details of why he chose this time of solitude, but it became apparent that, although confounding to his wife, it helped him prepare for his death.

I sat with the doctor several times in the weeks before he died. He seemed uncharacteristically steadfast, undaunted by what lay before him. During this time, he met with his son, who helped him build the coffin in which he was buried.

I am still moved when I recall how this man showed unusual solemnity in the face of death, and I cannot but think that the genuine grief he expressed over the harm he had caused his snake enabled him to come to terms with something long-denied in himself. In doing so, he realigned with an essential truth and found his courage.

For the ancient Greek priests and physicians who built the dream healing temples, the snake was a symbol for the sacred life force that can lift us up, make us strong, and restore vitality when we have been insulted by disease, suffered trauma, or forced to be untrue to ourselves. By aligning with our primal, instinctual nature, healing naturally occurs. Or the reverse may be true, too. If it is the time for the soul to shed its skin, then like the snake, without complaint and unperturbed, we might follow its wisdom and surrender to the great transition that leads to another life.

Our Overriding Intelligence

My mother never made peace with her serpent before she died. I am told by my brother, with whom she lived the last seven months of her life, that she continued to have those frightening nightmares, which has led me to ask, "What was it that persisted with my mother right to the very end?"

Being a deeply devoted fundamentalist Christian, my mother took the Bible literally and tried with great earnestness to live true to the mandates of her God. I remember that she even went beyond the example that Jesus had set and fasted for forty days, not once but twice. There seemed to be no sacrifice too great for her if it would help her fulfill the will of God.

But like with any virtue that is practiced to an extreme, my mother's piousness worked against her. In the previous chapter, I described how her dogmatic insistence that I follow her beliefs almost cost us our relationship. I also suspect that her preoccupation with being a good and obedient child of God, as well as a dutiful daughter, went against a primal intelligence in my mother, and it fashioned a commanding, countering presence in the form of the snake.

We all carry a deep intrinsic sense of right and wrong that is more elemental and foundational than even our chosen morality or spiritual ideals. It is the Law of Nature, the utter necessity and sacredness of *balance*. If we go against this by becoming extreme and one-sided, our bodies object through physical discomforts and disorders, and our dreams become conflictual. It's as if we have scales of justice in us established by our biology, and if one side becomes more weighted than the other, disruption follows.

My favorite of all quotes attributed to Carl Jung expresses this idea.

I would rather be whole than good[7].

Wholeness here refers to a state in which all the various potentials of our humanness work in harmony to help us live a full and meaningful life. Implied in Jung's words is a warning: even the virtue of goodness, like being gracious and kind to others, if pursued without consideration and respect for other aspects of nature, like fulfilling our basic needs, can derail us and lead to a lesser-lived life.

Indeed, there is something in us, which I will call an overriding intelligence (for lack of a better word), that looks out for us and even pushes back at us when we are in danger of losing contact with parts of us that are essential for our survival and fulfillment. It is this function that I suspect the serpent played in my mother's life. It is the preeminent symbol

---

7. Though widely seen on the web, this infamous quote is not in Jung's Collected Works and probably has its origins in Jung's correspondence or conversations. At the time of this writing, I could not trace its source..

of that part of our humanness that can resist, say no, and not succumb to any kind of pressure to give up the integrity of the self. The serpent that chased my mother may have been the most truthful, faithful part of her integrity that could resist an oppressive morality that was far too high and ideal for her to ever attain.

In Gratitude

Of course, I cannot complete my mother's nightmare for her. At best, I can only conjecture as to what the snake was for her. But given how riveting the serpent was for me as a close bystander, not only in my childhood but whenever I would visit my mother as an adult and hear her nightmares, I am compelled to come to terms with it for myself.

There is another reason I must answer the question that came to me early in life, "What does that snake want?" Some thirty years ago, I, too, encountered the snake, and like my mother, I was shaken.

In the dream, I walked outside the front door of my home and saw an enormously large snake stretched across the walkway. This in itself would have been uncanny enough to alarm me, but what pierced me to the heart was that the snake already had within its mouth and halfway down its throat something very precious to me, my beloved cat, Isabella.

If you are not an animal lover, this story will not have the emotional weight it will for someone who has formed emotional bonds with their so-called pet. Isabella was, for me, a companion. I found her in an animal shelter just before she was to be euthanized. Though I technically rescued her, it was she who saved me during an intensely lonely period of my life. Her companionship was constant, unequivocally warm, and took the edge off an isolation painful to bear.

Seeking to understand the seemingly violent dream, I asked, "Why would Nature be killing off another part of itself?" I was confounded.

As I have done countless times over the years, I began my study of this dream by calling on the investigative method *Distill the Essence*. Here I sought to understand the essential qualities of my cat. "What is it about my dear Isabella," I asked, "that would be considered a liability and thus in need of being taken away?"

The most distinguishing quality about the cat was that she was unusually related to humans. Even my friends noted this about her. Whenever we went for walks on the country road where I lived, Isabella followed us. Inside the house, she was almost certain to move to whatever room I occupied. Although heartwarming, this high degree of relatedness also caused her to suffer. Whenever I walked down to my boat on the small pond to take it for a row, Isabella predictably trailed me, but she would not get in the boat even if I tried to coax her. When I pulled away from land without her, she would erupt into the most haunting howling protest I have ever heard. They were loud, pitiful moans that could be heard for a full minute or more to the other side of the pond, seeming to express both alarm and grief.

It seemed that Isabella had lost some of her wildness. Lacking her natural animal autonomy, she would become highly distressed. But what did this have to do with me?

Being a young psychologist at the time, just when many books were being published on addiction, I asked, "Am I codependent? Is my well-being and sense of self fragilely based on how well a significant other is relating to me?" The idea seemed consistent with the dream, but I did not feel an affinity for such an interpretation. I regarded myself as being independent. After all, I was in my early forties, had never married nor stayed in a romantic relationship much longer than a year, so it seemed I was a highly autonomous man.

The dream did not agree. Through the image of Isabella, I was shown a side of myself that, to put it mildly, needed to be addressed. At the time, however, I could not and did not want to see this. It would take several years and a great deal of suffering before I realized that isolating myself, cutting myself off from vulnerable feelings, and attempting not to need anyone had more to do with pseudo-independence than it did with the deep autonomy that is characteristic of the snake.

Gradually, however, I came to recognize myself as the anguished Isabella languishing at the side of the pond. As I ventured deeper into friendships and romantic involvements, I would sometimes experience a similar panic whenever important relationships were threatened. I did not know what to make of this, but it was a profoundly painful state, something I had managed to avoid earlier in my life by being isolative and emotionally guarded.

Once, while undergoing a therapeutic psychedelic session, I traced this anguish of separation back to my first eight days after birth. I was born in a distressing condition that resulted in my being placed in "an incubator" while my mother was sent home to rest. I don't know if this early experience was causative of my later "Isabella states," or if it was simply a truthful metaphor for my inner condition of not having access to my own internal mothering capacities. Regardless, the threat of separation was difficult to bear.

For years, whenever I thought about my dream, I found it much easier to be concerned with the cat than the snake. Of course, this was because my psychological condition was more akin to my anguished Isabella than it was to the snake. The serpent was foreign, eerie, and unlike anything I knew in myself. Eventually, however, I became curious. "What is this serpentine capacity like?" I finally asked. "What part of me does it symbolize?"

My dream of the snake pointed me to a capacity I knew little of at the time but one which I came to appreciate as the result of learning more about trauma and its resolution. The snake showed me how to meet the panicked states into which I would sometimes fall. Such profound vulnerabilities are not remedied by avoiding them as I had done for years through my hyper-independence. Instead, we heal them by contacting them, courageously feeling pain with compassion and a degree of fortitude. In this way, we become intimate with the suffering, not shunning it. As the snake did not back away from the anguished Isabella, so we too can taste our suffering, no longer repelled by it, and thus neutralize it.

For me, my snake is symbolic of an instinctual steadiness that is not repelled or overcome by suffering. When we concurrently occupy this capacity while also allowing the experience of pain, we digest distress, take it in thoroughly, and thus *metabolize* it, an idea in trauma work that refers to a process of neutralizing painful experiences. To do this, we must practice dual awareness, essentially being both the cat and snake, circulating consciousness back and forth between them. In this way, suffering is transformed.

At the time of the dream, now three decades ago, I was not familiar with the deep steadiness that the snake symbolizes. Yes, I was a meditator and could sit lengthy periods without flinching, but unbeknownst to me, I was using spiritual practice to disassociate, to avoid pain. Of course, the snake does none of this. It doesn't fly above the earth. Its belly touches the ground. It is earthen power and can remind us of our capacity to touch all things here and within our bodies.

Today I no longer use meditation or any spiritual practice to escape. I now utilize the calming breath to steady myself to listen to what is felt in the body. Often I find disturbances. My body is tense. I am not initially sure why, but I question it, "Now what disturbs you?" Depending on the hour and the day, I discover many valuable things. A conflicted relationship may be in need of my attention. I may feel anxious about an upcoming appointment and thus must get better prepared. I may just as well feel sadness over climate change. This, too, requires a creative response from me. The physical and emotional bodies provide enormous information, and if listened to, can be a remarkable source of guidance.

There is one other aspect of the serpent's power I must mention. It has to do with our deepest instinct for survival, self-preservation, and the will to live. We are equipped by Nature with deep instinctual powers, which in essence orient us to pursue what is pleasurable and life-giving and to resist that which is oppressive, confining, and inhibiting of life. If these powerful capacities are dampened and disavowed, we become compromised and weakened, leading us to assume that we must equivocate to have the dependency on others thought necessary to survive. Such was my condition as the anguished, fearful Isabella.

Quoting Carl Jung (Dunn, 2015),

> We fear our serpent.

By this, I think Jung recognized that our instinctual capacities are so fierce and strong that if we let ourselves know them fully, we would become afraid, for indeed the pure force of life is disruptive to anything untrue and antithetical to life.

Unfortunately, much of our early survival and stability often depends upon making strategic sacrifices, compromises, hiding our uniqueness, and denying our authentic nature to avoid punishment, rejection, and shame. In the process, we move further away from our instinctual nature.

Yet, this fundamental life force remains within us. It is our inherent resiliency. A formidable way to connect with this power is through dream images, but not just by interpreting them; instead, by imagining and feeling ourselves to be them. In this case, I have called on the steady, wild, instinctual power of the serpent inside me countless times, especially when I have been shaken, afraid, and threatened with the loss of a relationship or intimidating economic, health, or career challenges. When connecting to the healing image—be it a primal warrior, bear, snake, or any other dream figure gifted to me—I immediately find strength not ordinarily available to me. Living with images in this visceral way, allowing myself to feel what it is like to be something greater than what I have known myself to be, has gradually expanded my identity. I am no longer just the fearful one, threatened by loss. Another presence in me is capable of navigating the most turbulent of seas. Such is the gift of dreams.

Though my mother could not welcome the serpent, I now wish to pay gratitude for this reviled part of Nature, our nature. It is our uncorrupted power, so fiercely independent, sovereign, and astute that it sometimes scares us. To benefit from this gift of heaven, we must turn and face it. Looking into its eyes, we may recognize it as an almost forgotten intelligence within ourselves: courageous, resilient, and far more brilliant than what we have thought ourselves to be. It is out of tender mercy that something in us dreams this. Frightening and off-putting at first, it is the opposite of what we want but proves upon deep reflection to be the very thing we most need.

Where
to Go
from Here

Before closing this book, I wish to suggest two ways to gain greater wisdom from your dreams.

Become Familiar with the Investigative Methods of Dreamwork

How to Complete a Nightmare is an expansion of a chapter from another book of mine, *Your Dream's Ten Best Friends: Essential Guiding Principles that Reveal the Truth of Your Dreams*. In this book, I discuss ten principles that I follow when I study a dream. One of these guiding principles relates to nightmares, and it is presented as a piece of advice: *Always Complete a Nightmare*. In other words, don't leave a nightmare as it occurred, but rather bring it to resolution. Given the complexity and distressing intensity of nightmares, I felt more was needed than a single chapter on the subject. Therefore, I added stories and enlarged the original chapter to stand alone as its own book.

Each of the *Ten Best Friends* is a succinct piece of advice meant to guide the dreamer to discover the unique significance of a dream. There are no predetermined, overly-generalized suggestions given about dream symbols. Instead, by following each of the ten investigative principles, dreamers gradually and organically discover the dream's unique relevance for them.

If you are interested in learning the investigative methods of dreamwork that I typically use when I study a dream, I recommend that you find your way to *Your Dream's Ten Best Friends*. An excerpt of this book can be found on my website: www.evolutionarydreaming.com.

I have published *How to Complete a Nightmare* to be a companion for my film, *Dreaming to Heal PTSD and Moral Injury*. I anticipate that many viewers of this film will want more information to enable them to work with their own disturbing dreams. If you have not yet seen this film, I recommend doing so. It tells the story of a traumatized Iraqi war vet who found healing by understanding the purpose of his nightmares. Additionally, the film illustrates how I use some of the investigative methods described in *Your Dream's Ten Best Friends*.

Find Someone to Explore Your Dreams with You

Following this chapter, I make several suggestions for further reading. However, I must say that while some books about dreams are undoubtedly helpful, they pale in comparison to having a skilled dream worker work with your dreams. Over the years, when discussing dreams with my mentor, I have learned far more in any single session than what a dozen books about dreams have taught me. Thus, I highly recommend finding a skilled listener with whom you can discuss your dreams. Whether such a person is a trained psychotherapist or not, consider these suggestions when looking for someone to help you.

- Beware of someone so tied to a particular theory that they immediately tell you what your dream means. Instead, look for someone who will *explore* and *investigate* a dream with you. My warning pertains to both dream interpretation from traditional cultures that often have fixed ideas about symbolism, as well as modern theories like Freudian or even Jungian psychology, from which I have learned a great deal. Guard against anyone who flippantly or dogmatically shoves your dreams into predetermined categories without patiently and respectfully listening not only to you but to your *dream figures* (see below).
- Prefer someone who will help you talk with dream figures. By this, I am referring to Active Imagination, a method of investigation that I have also discussed in this book as *Let Dream Presences Speak*. Often the dream itself does not provide adequate information to give a satisfying understanding of its intention. Additional information needs to be obtained. A skillful dream worker will help you pose questions to dream figures and encourage you to imagine what they wish to say in return. Such imaginative dialogue is where the gold lies.

• Do not settle for quick explanations about the meaning of your dream unless, of course, it gets right to the heart of the matter, and you are left surprised and satisfied. When exploring the significance of a dream, follow one of the guiding principles I write about in *Your Dream's Ten Best Friends*: Insist on Surprise. Favor interpretations that are unexpected, not ideas with which you are already familiar.

• The best and most truthful interpretations are those that affect you *emotionally*. An emotional response may result from discovering an inspiring idea that leads you to adopt a new attitude or behavior, or, conversely, a dream may bring you to a realization that sobers you, asking that you change something about how you live your life. Unfortunately, most interpretations I observe people settling for are usually *explanations* about why they dreamed such and such. The dreamer remains unaffected. For example, someone may conclude, "Oh, I dreamed of an elephant chasing me because I saw a movie last week about the circus." But I ask, "Might the elephant be symbolic of your need to persist and overcome seemingly impossible obstacles?" In my view, the purpose of dreaming is to evolve us, to change us so that we are wiser and more skillful for the challenges of life. In this sense, dreams don't repeat what we already know or replay a trite incident from waking life. Instead, an important realization is being called for. When you find this, you are likely to receive a confirmation of your discovery with a felt sense of "Aha!" If you have not yet felt this, continue looking.

———————

The years when I was pursuing my inner images were the most important in my life—in them everything essential was decided.
CARL JUNG[8]

———————

8. Quote from Jung's memoir (1989), *Memories, Dreams, Reflections*, page 199.

Resources and Recommended Reading

Cartwright, R. D. (1996). Dreams and adaptation to divorce. In D. Barrett (Ed.), *Trauma and dreams* (pp. 179–185). Harvard University Press.

Davis, J.L. (2008) *Treating Post-Trauma Nightmares: A Cognitive-Behavioral Approach.* Spring Publishing Company

> This is not an inspirational self-help book, though I found the research presented here to inspire hope in me. It is written for professionals who wish to learn how to implement a program for nightmare sufferers using Image Rehearsal Therapy. Clear and concise.

Dunn, C. (2015). *Carl Jung: Wounded Healer of the Soul.* Watkins Publishing.

> There are several biographies on Carl Jung, but this is my favorite. Dunn's book is not exhaustive by any means, but she captures pivotal moments in Jung's life by providing exemplary pictures and memorable quotes by him.

Arthur, G. & Arthur, E.(2014). *The Mythology of Eden.* Hamilton Books.

> This book is a formidable study of why Western civilization's most popular and enduring creation story was written. It has been essential in helping me understand the rich history of serpent symbolism as I wrote the chapter *Why the Serpent Chased My Mother.*

Dispenza, J. (2014). *You Are the Placebo.* Hay House, Inc.

Hannah, B. (1981), *Encounters with the Soul: Active Imagination as Developed by C.G. Jung*. Chiron Publications

> *The most valuable part of this book for me has been chapter one, in which Barbara Hannah, a close associate of Carl Jung, speaks of the importance of standing your ground with dream figures, or as she says, "having it out" with a dream. Even though I have quoted from this book, it is not the most accessible for beginners if you are looking to learn more about Active Imagination, a method of dream investigation that I have referred to as Let Dream Presences Speak. For an easier read on this subject, I suggest Robert Johnson's (1986) lovely book, Inner Work: Using Dreams and Active Imagination for Personal Growth.*

Johnson, R. (1986). *Inner Work: Using Dreams and Active Imagination for Personal Growth*. Harper San Francisco.

> *For those looking for practical guidance on working with their dreams, Inner Work has been the book I have most recommended. Johnson, in characteristic form, has taken one of Carl Jung's concepts, Active Imagination, and made it more accessible for the general public without over-simplifying the material.*

Jung, C. (1989), *Memories, Dreams, Reflections*. Vintage Publishers

> *I have re-read Carl Jung's autobiography, Memories, more than any other book because I love Jung's transparency about his struggles and how he came to develop his way of working with dreams. This memoir does not fall into the easy-to-read how-to genre of self-help books. Nevertheless, it is filled with jewels of wisdom.*

Jung, C. (1968). *Man and His Symbols*. Dell Publishing Co., Inc.

> *While many books summarize Jung's ideas, I especially love this one expressly written for the general public, authored by Jung himself and three of his colleagues. Of note is Marie-Louise von Franz's chapter on the individuation process. It is one of the best descriptions I have read on how we continue to change and evolve over a lifetime.*

Kessler, D. 2019). *Finding Meaning: The Sixth Stage of Grief*. Scribner.

Van der Kolk, B. (2014). The Body Keeps the Score: Brain, Mind, and Body in the Healing of Trauma. Viking Press.

> Arguably, The Body Keeps the Score is currently the most sobering and influential book in our culture to help us understand the lingering effects of trauma.

Krakow, B & Zadra, A. (2006) "Clinical Management of Chronic Nightmares: Imagery Rehearsal Therapy." Behavioral Sleep Medicine, 4(1), 45–70.

Krakow, B. & Zadra, A. (2010). "Image Rehearsal Therapy: Principles and Practice." Sleep Medicine Clinics journal published by Elsevier.

> This succinct and accessible article provides an overview of IRT. It first appeared in a professional journal and can now be found at https:// antoniozadra.com/sites/default/files/biblio/krakow_zadra.sleep_med_clinics.pdf.

> For a more thorough understanding of Karkow's work with Image Rehearsal Therapy, see his book, along with Joseph Neidhart (1992), Conquering Bad Dreams and Nightmares: A Guide to Understand, Interpretation, and Cure. Note: The non-interpretative method of working with nightmares presented here is unlike what I have presented in How to Complete a Nightmare.

Levine, P. (2008). Healing Trauma: A Pioneering Program for Restoring the Wisdom of Your Body. Sounds True.

Litz, Lebowitz, Gray, & Nash (2015). Adaptive Disclosure: A New Treatment for Military Trauma, Loss, and Moral Injury. The Guilford Press.

> There are numerous books on moral injury. I have listed this one because it shows in practical terms how trauma from injury to conscience can and must be approached differently than what is typically done with fear-based trauma. This is an excellent book intended for psychotherapists who wish to be more nuanced in their treatment of the various forms of PTSD.

Mate, G. (2003). When the Body Says No: Understanding the Stress-Disease Connection. Wiley.

Miller, A. (2001). *The Truth Will Set You Free: Overcoming Emotional Blindness and Finding Your True Adult Self.* Basic Books.

> *Miller's bold and penetrating analysis helped me understand how the authors of the Garden of Eden creation story likely suffered abuse as children by their autocratic fathers. Her insight was helpful in me in writing the last dream story, Why the Serpent Chased My Mother. Miller's many other books, most notably For Your Own Good: Hidden Cruelty in Child-Rearing and the Roots of Violence (1983) and The Body Keeps the Score: The Lingering Effects of Hurtful Parenting (2014), have been decisive in helping me experience empathy for my childhood and that of others.*

Miller, A. (1983). *For Your Own Good: Hidden Cruelty in Child-rearing and the Roots of Violence.* Farrar, Straus, Giroux.

New International Version (1978). Biblica.

North, M. (2002). "Greek Medicine: The Hippocratic Oath." Library of Medicine. https://www.nlm.nih.gov/hmd/greek/greek_oath.html

Revonsuo, A. (2000). "The reinterpretation of dreams: An evolutionary hypothesis of the function of dreaming." Behavioral and Brain Sciences, Volume 23, Issue 6, pp. 877-901, December 2000.

Tick, E. (2001). *The Practice of Dream Healing: Bringing Ancient Greek Mysteries into Modern Medicine.* Quest Books.

> *This book inspired me to visit the site of one of the largest dream healing temple complexes of ancient Greece. People across the ancient world once traveled great distances to such places to sleep in sacred dream incubation chambers to find healing. Tick reminds us that modern Western medicine had its origins in these ancient temples. The author shows the relevance of these remarkable mind-body practices by describing his work with traumatized war veterans.*

Walker, M. (2017). *Why We Sleep: Unlocking the Power of Sleep and Dreams.* Scribner.

> You will never want to miss a good night's sleep after reading this book. In addition to listing the many health benefits of sleep, the author provides an easy-to-read summary of the emotional and memory-enhancing functions that occur during dreaming.

Acknowledgments

My mother, Evelyn Worley, has, without doubt, played the most decisive role in this book being written. Little did she know that the nightmares she suffered, which disrupted my sleep as well as hers, would become my initiation into a lifelong search to understand dreaming.

Dearest of friends, Jasmine Singh, more than anyone I know, courageously tested my early concepts of Nightmare Completion with her own dreams. Her fortitude to face what was frightening not only inspired me but also gave me invaluable feedback that helped me refine my ideas about how to bring disturbing dreams to completion.

Sukie Colegrave (sukiecolegrave.com), therapist and author, who has patiently and empathically worked with hundreds of my dreams over three decades, has by example taught me the subtleties of elegant dreamwork. Without her, this book could not have been written.

My brother and sister-in-law Mark and Ramona Worley helped keep me afloat with their financial gifts during a lengthy nomadic writer's retreat, believing in me before reading one word of this book. They also provided the funds for this book and my film, *Dreaming to Heal PTSD and Moral Injury*, to be marketed, without which few people would learn of this material.

I express my appreciation to my primary editor Lily Sepha, who has the unusual talent of suggesting edits with finesse and grace, a sure gift for a first-time writer. Her elegant editorial skills have not only helped refine me as a writer, but just as importantly, she has evoked confidence in me.

Psychotherapists and best of friends, Barbara Cernak and Robert Sand-cucci, with whom I have shared many of my dreams over the years, were the readers I most turned to whenever I needed to assess how the concepts of Nightmare Completion would appear to seasoned therapists, which they are. Not only that, they provided lodging (and gourmet meals) when the first draft of this book was written.

Ana-Agei Clothiaux, a long-standing friend with whom I have shared many dreams and a dream worker in her own right, read many of my stories and was the consummate encourager, reminding me that the wisdom in Nightmare Completion was sorely needed.

I express appreciation for Pakistani artist Muhammad Ahsan Ayaz, known on Fiverr.com as *Artholistic*. His insightful imagination gave visual expression to most of the dream illustrations of this book. He is a talented illustrator whose work is also featured in my film *Dreaming to Heal PTSD and Moral Injury*.

Jocelyn Audet Pierce, Somatic Practitioner, not only read drafts of this book, but she also provided me my first writing sanctuary on her beautiful farm in Virginia when I first started this book.

Margaretta McIlvaine, encouraging presence par excellence, graciously gave me shelter at her gorgeous retreat center, Bridge Between the Worlds, during an extended writer's retreat. Her meditative pond is the most potent in rural Virginia.

With astute editorial eyes, Rebecca Raskin played a crucial role when she read one of the later drafts of this book and gave me a thumbs-up to publish.

Don West, a longtime friend with whom I have shared countless dreams, did the tedious finishing edits on this book.

I wish to thank Delaney Covelli (delaneycovelli.com) for her thoughtful work in creating the trailer for this book. She did the unexpected by producing a gentle and inviting video introduction to a frightening subject.

Susie Schaefer (finishthebookpublishing.com), the consummate inspiring publishing consultant, played a decisive role in helping me navigate near-overwhelming details as a first-time self-published writer. Working with Susie, Michelle M. White (mmwbooks.com) formatted this book, finessed the book cover, and beautified the written word.

Finally, I will forever remember the dreamers who have allowed me to use their intimate experiences in dreams for this book.

About the Author

Len Worley received his Ph.D. in counseling psychology in 1981 and has worked as a psychologist, marriage and family therapist, Rolfing body-worker, and as a researcher and mentor in dream studies. He currently produces films, writes and publishes books, and offers training and consultations related to dreams and depth psychology.

You can learn more about Dr. Worley and his work at
www.evolutionarydreaming.com.

Lightning Source UK Ltd.
Milton Keynes UK
UKHW022306160522
403082UK00006B/456

9 798985 291000